THE Simply REAL HEALTH COOKBOOK

by **SARAH ADLER**

creator of simplyrealhealth.com

Easy real food recipes for a healthy life, made simple.

PHOTOGRAPHED BY
JASMINE NICOLE PULLEY

DESIGNED BY
KRISTIN McCLEEREY

The Simply Real Health Cookbook by Sarah Adler

Copyright © 2015 by Sarah Adler

All rights reserved. Published 2015. No part of this publication may be reproduced, distributed, or transmitted in any form or by any means, including photocopying, recording, or other electronic or mechanical methods, without the prior written permission of the publisher, except in the case of brief quotations embodied in critical reviews and certain other noncommercial uses permitted by copyright law.

ISBN-13: 978-0-692-33138-5

Printed in South Korea
by Star Print Brokers, Inc.
Bellevue, WA
StarPrintBrokers.com

Second Printing.

Ordering Information:
Quantity sales. Special discounts are available on quantity purchases by corporations, associations, and others. For permission requests or ordering information, visit: simplyrealhealth.com/contact.

Prop Stylist: Jasmine Pulley

Back cover and copyright page photos: Carina Skrobecki

DEDICATION

*For my sweet family, dear friends, and the entire Simply Real Health community: this book is for you. Thank you for years of incredible support, encouragement, and love. From my heart, soul, and little kitchen to yours, let this book be a tiny thank you for all that you give to me. You all inspire **me** so much every single day, and a project like this would not be a reality without you. I hope it brings you years of amazing and vibrant health, happiness, and the best of memories around your table, with those you love the most.*

TABLE OF CONTENTS

INTRODUCTION 6

PANTRY STAPLES 14

HELPFUL TOOLS & GADGETS 17

WHAT IS REAL FOOD? 18

A DAY IN THE LIFE 20

STRATEGIES FOR THE WEEK 22

Breakfast + Anytime Green Smoothies 26

Other Breakfast + Brunch Ideas 42

Make Ahead Dishes 66

Entrée Salads 110

Soups 142

Main Meals 172

Vegetables + Sides 236

Appetizers 262

Snacks 280

Sauces + Dressings 294

Cocktails 328

Desserts 346

EXTRA LOVE + THANK YOUS 364

INDEX 366

> "WHAT IF YOU JUST LEARNED HOW TO EAT BETTER OVERALL? DAILY AND MINDFULLY. AND HERE'S THE GORGEOUS PART: WITHOUT THE NEED TO BE PERFECT.

INTRODUCTION

About Simply Real Health: A Little Background

I started Simply Real Health because I wanted to teach people how to live a healthier lifestyle. Daily. As in, during the course of normal, every day life.

Not life on a juice cleanse or diet program, with strict rules and *yes* foods and *no* foods. And not life where you completely give up caring about eating healthy, either. You know, the "screw it, I'm just going to eat a cupcake" mentality.

Because—although real for a lot of people—these are the extremes. *Health* seen in black and white, when we are either being crazily health-conscious or totally NOT at all. Or one or the other, or maybe back and forth between the two, depending on the week or the year. But, it doesn't work. And it actually makes things a lot harder than they need to be.

Because of one little thing: real life happens in the gray zone.

And when it comes to being healthy, throwing away those extreme rules is radical, weird, and uncomfortable. As humans, we crave rules and structure. We want *good* and *bad* foods. We want the easy, definitive answer.

To follow the latest study or jump on the new bandwagon diet. We want a silver bullet and perfection. Or to not think about it at all.

Here's the problem though: life is messy and imperfect. Beautifully messy. And when we live in real life (apart from a few successful days of suffering through a cayenne pepper-and-lemon juice cleanse or steamed chicken and broccoli only stint), the black and white rules about our food and health really don't work. Especially long term. Aka, for the rest of your life.

So, I set out to welcome people to the beautiful gray zone. Because, although it took me a long time to get here, I happen to love it here.

It's a place where, instead of rigidly adhering to rules, and then madly and shamefully failing when real life events come up, you just learn how to eat better overall. Daily. Mindfully. And here's the gorgeous part: without the need to be perfect.

So that eating mostly well becomes your default. And a happy thing that you want to do daily because it happens to make you feel really, really

About Simply Real Health: A Little Background (continued)

good. It's not something that you accomplish and check boxes and are done—it's a lifestyle shift.

Enter my fiery mission with Simply Real Health:

To teach people how to eat. In a healthy and simple way. That happily works in the context of real daily life, not against it.

Because a healthy lifestyle is actually pretty simple, but in a confusing world of food marketing, diets, energy bars, and nonfat this-and-that, it feels anything but simple.

Every single day we are inundated with a constant stream of media about health food. We hear about miracle programs and supplements. We read about antioxidants, carbohydrates, cholesterol, and the right kind of fats.

In the frenzy, we have forgotten how to just be normal about eating well. Or, the bigger problem, none us were ever taught the basics on how to eat well to begin with.

Even though—are you ready for a little truth bomb? Healthy eating directly affects nearly everything in our lives. It affects how we feel, how we look, how we sleep, our mood, our confidence, our productivity, our relationships, etc. The list goes on. But what if we were never taught how to eat healthily, or live healthily on a general level? Like what a healthy lifestyle even means at 11 am on a Monday morning or sitting on a plane or making dinner tomorrow night?

That's why I started Simply Real Health. I wanted to teach people about healthy food in a meaningful, real-life-in-the-gray-zone sort of way.

I've got no agenda, no diet plan, and no one is paying me under the table to pitch a pill to you. My sole desire is to educate you about what healthy food is, where to find it, and how to make it simple enough to actually work into your real life. Daily. Consistently. And as your new normal.

Because when you do this, a crazy thing happens. You start to feel good.

No, you start to feel great. And when you feel great, you can handle life a whole lot better. With more ease, more joy and more freedom. Less extremes. Less guilt. Steady, balanced, and calm.

And then everything else in life gets so much better too.

So that's my jam. To show people that you can eat better, keep things simple and easy, but also enjoy the really good parts of life in the process and have a healthy relationship to really good food.

> ENTER MY FIERY MISSION WITH SIMPLY REAL HEALTH: TO TEACH PEOPLE HOW TO EAT. IN A HEALTHY AND SIMPLE WAY. THAT HAPPILY WORKS IN THE CONTEXT OF REAL DAILY LIFE, NOT AGAINST IT.

Why I Wrote This Book

I wrote this cookbook because I love feeling good. And, want to know my secret weapon? Feeling good comes from eating well over time.

So, if we're on the same page about that, that leads up to the next question: what's for dinner then? And lunch? And everything in between? Specifically and food wise? How do we take the concept of eating more real, whole food and fit it into our daily lives?

So, that's reason number one. To share what I do, what I've taught my clients and blog readers to do, and give you a real tangible way to start upgrading your lifestyle. All in one book.

But, secondly, I have a confession. I have so many cookbooks. So many. I bought a lot of them early on in my healthy eating journey. For inspiration, to learn techniques and different theories. Or, purely just to drool over the pictures. But, whenever I went to actually cook from them, I started to notice something weird—I couldn't get myself to take that next step, to actually start cooking.

I had "healthy" cookbooks: vegan or vegetarian maybe. Or some older hippie ones I found at Goodwill. Each recipe with the longest list of ingredients you ever did see or brimming with obscure, exotic ingredients that were hard to find or something I'd never use again. Or recipes with way too much soy or processed health foods.

I'd look through them, but never actually make the recipes, because I'm somewhat of a lazy cook, truth be told. I don't enjoy spending an hour on a single dish, no matter what the occasion is, especially for a normal, everyday dinner.

Then, there were my cookbooks that said they were for "fast" or "easy" meals, but were almost 85% pasta or bread based dishes. Which—hello—won't make anyone feel great.

It was rare to find a recipe that was healthy (meaning real-food based), simple (ingredient-wise), and easy (meaning not time-intensive). Which is why I started to write my own. Out of necessity I guess. And a little craftiness. Which is where Simply Real Health even got started—as a sweet little food blog.

And after a few years, I had so many recipes, and people kept asking for more. Because, as it turned out, most people were like me—busy, wanting to eat healthy and feel great, but didn't want to spend hours of their day doing so.

Rinse and repeat for 7 years, and I ended up with a lot of recipes. Over 400. And there were multiple rising stars. The dishes that everyone loved, and commented on, or told me that it had changed their opinion (or their kid's or husband's opinion) of healthy food and healthy eating, or had revolutionized their dinner, breakfast, or lunch routine.

So, this cookbook is my collection of these very favorites. The game changers. The creative ways to get more vegetables in your life. And the easiest path to feeling better in a daily real-life perspective.

I wrote this cookbook because I believe you can have it all with healthy food—food that tastes great, makes you feel great, looks beautiful, and is quick and easy. Using good quality and simple ingredients. So that you can live a healthy lifestyle without all the extra hassle. It's a healthy life, made simple.

How To Use This Book:

For beginners: follow the recipe as written. It will turn out amazing, guaranteed.

For more advanced cooks: check out my notes on each recipe for inspiration on how to modify or tweak the dishes to your liking.

For everyone: please don't be afraid of messing up. The beauty of using such fresh and pure ingredients is that you don't need to do much to make them taste great. I want you to take these recipes, practice with them, play with them and make them your own!

Anyone can cook these dishes. I am not a chef. My knife skills are still terrible. And, I didn't even learn to cook until my early twenties. If I can do it, you can do it.

You'll also see these helpful icons throughout the book to guide your inspiration:

 GLUTEN FREE   1-POT MEAL

 DAIRY FREE   ENTERTAINING

 VEGETARIAN   QUICK MEAL

 MAKE-AHEAD   KID-FRIENDLY

What You'll Notice:

There are so many vegetable dishes in this book! Out of everything, that is always my first goal: to get more people to eat more vegetables....and like it. Throughout this book, there are so many different and creative ways you can incorporate more vegetables into your life without existing solely on salads. Although there are plenty of ideas in that realm too.

The biggest section in this book is the "Make-Ahead Dishes". On purpose. This is how you can start eating healthier without all the extra time. These are the gold gems, and what I make most often in my own kitchen and life.

Most ingredients found here can be found in any grocery store to make it approachable for everyone to eat better, no matter where you live or shop. Any exceptions to this can be found in the **Pantry + Staples** section. This book is very food-sensitivity-friendly. All of the recipes listed are made with 100% whole, real food and nothing processed. Because everyone deserves to eat good food.

> ALL OF THE RECIPES LISTED ARE MADE WITH 100% WHOLE, REAL FOOD AND NOTHING PROCESSED.

PANTRY STAPLES

Unrefined, extra-virgin coconut oil: This amazing and nutrient rich oil is great for high-heat cooking (think pan-fried meats and veggies, or in delicious recipes like the **Coconut Oil Popcorn**). Plus, it has great healthy fat to support better digestion, energy, metabolism, and less inflammation all around. It can even double as a pure body and face lotion! Each brand has a slightly different taste, so experiment to find a flavor profile you like best.

Organic, extra-virgin olive oil: Spanish, Italian, and Greek varieties of olive oil each have their own flavor profiles, so experimenting with a few until you find your favorite is a great idea. I buy one larger, less expensive bottle (but still organic and extra-virgin) to use for roasting and cooking, and one smaller, more expensive bottle to eat raw on salads and drizzled over veggies. There is definitely a taste difference—you get what you pay for in this category, so choose wisely!

Organic, grass-fed butter: Contrary to popular belief, organic grass fed butter is a very healthy thing to use in your kitchen, when it's sourced well. Plus, it's amazing over vegetables, meat, grains and anything cooked at a high temperature. Don't be afraid to use butter to enhance great, nutritionally-dense foods like veggies instead of reserving it only for something less so, like pasta.

Unrefined toasted sesame oil: This oil is great for drizzling over your food right before serving. I use it in place of soy sauce for an easy soy and gluten free umami replacement.

Pantry Staples (continued)

Flours
- Almond flour + almond meal
- Cornmeal
- Brown rice flour
- Gluten free flour blend
- Coconut flour

Vinegars
- Balsamic vinegar:
- Unfiltered or raw apple cider vinegar
- Red wine vinegar
- White wine vinegar
- Sherry vinegar

Sweeteners
- Organic raw honey
- Organic maple syrup, grade b
- Organic blackstrap molasses

Canned
- Garbanzo beans
- White beans
- Black beans
- Tomatoes
- Tuna, wild
- Coconut milk
- Organic chicken or vegetable stock

Condiments
- Dijon mustard
- Organic ketchup
- Anchovy paste
- Hot sauce
- Tamari sauce
- Truffle oil
- Sundried tomatoes
- Tomato paste

Whole Grains
- Quinoa
- Brown rice
- Wild rice
- Millet
- Polenta
- Steel cut oats

Nuts
- Cashews
- Walnuts
- Pistachios
- Almonds
- Macadamia nuts
- Peanut butter
- Almond butter
- Tahini
- Sesame seeds
- Pumpkin seeds
- Chia seeds

Dried Fruit
- Dates
- Raisins
- Mangos

From The fridge
- Grass-fed butter
- Raw parmesan cheese
- Goat cheese
- Feta cheese
- Lemons
- Limes
- Olives
- Onion
- Garlic
- Eggs

Most Used/ Favorite Spices + Seasonings
- Sea salt
- Pepper
- Garam masala
- Cinnamon
- Curry powder
- Smoked paprika
- Italian herb blend

Helpful TOOLS + GADGETS

CHECK OUT THE RESOURCE PAGE ON THE SIMPLY REAL HEALTH WEBSITE FOR A LIST OF MY FAVORITE BRANDS + DIRECT LINKS TO THE ONES I LOVE AND RECCOMMEND!

- ◇ Blender
- ◇ Cast iron pan
- ◇ Crockpot
- ◇ Enameled soup pot
- ◇ Good paring knife
- ◇ Good chopping knife
- ◇ Spiralizer
- ◇ Mandoline
- ◇ Zester/Grater
- ◇ Citrus juicer
- ◇ Baking sheets
- ◇ Parchment paper
- ◇ Glass storage containers

REAL FOODS ARE SIMPLE FOODS, PURE FOODS + WHOLE FOODS. THERE ARE 12 BASIC TYPES:

Vegetables: any and as many as you can.

Fruit: fresh or dried.

Nuts + Seeds: any kind is great: walnuts, cashews, peanuts, almonds, pistachios, sesame seeds, sunflower seeds, etc. Raw is best, then dry roasted. Stay away from those with oils, added flavorings or sugars.

Beans + Legumes + Lentils: canned or dry beans that you soak and cook on your own.

Eggs: organic, free range are best. Scrambled, poached, fried, fritattas or omelettes are all great options, even for dinner.

Poultry: Ideally organic or naturally raised. Chicken and turkey are the most common sources.

Meat: Ideally organic or naturally raised. Beef, lamb, pork, bison and buffalo products.

Seafood: Fish, shellfish and crustaceans. Wild is much better than farm-raised.

Dairy: Ideally organic or naturally raised and whole milk versions only.

Grains: Whole grain versions you soak and cook in water, or sprouted grain products. Quinoa, brown rice, organic corn products, steel cut oats and millet are the most common naturally gluten free sources of whole grains.

Naturally Occuring Healthy Fats: unrefined coconut oil, organic grass-fed butter, extra virgin olive oil + toasted unrefined sesame oil.

Naturally Occuring Sweeteners: organic grade b maple syrup, raw honey or blackstrap molasses.

What is Not "Real Food"?

NOT REAL FOOD IS PRETTY MUCH EVERYTHING ELSE:

◇ Processed foods

◇ Food products with long ingredients lists

◇ Things that you can't pronounce in the ingredient list

◇ Things that say/brag they are good for you on the front label

◇ Things that don't exist in nature/ man-made food products or were only created in the last 50 years

◇ Artificial sugars, weird oils, chemicals, preservatives or toxins

A DAY IN THE LIFE

I'm going to tell you a secret that I rarely tell anyone. Most days, I eat two meals a day. Lunch and dinner. I know. It freaks people out, but I'm not starving or depriving myself, I promise, I'm just eating when I'm hungry. I can do this (and have great energy) because I eat nutrient dense, real, whole food.

Here's the thing: real food naturally balances your blood sugar and keeps

THE SIMPLY REAL HEALTH COOKBOOK | *Easy real food recipes for a healthy life, made simple.*

it steady throughout the day, so you don't need as much food as you might be accustomed to eating. Everything I eat gives something to my body instead of taking energy away from it, like processed food does. It's more productive eating, really.

And on a bigger scale, the result is that I think about food less but enjoy it way more. So my relationship to food is better because of it, and I trust my body and its signals more. And, my meals are awesome. Hearty is a good word for them. Maybe even luscious. Sometimes I get looks at restaurants or at people's houses, "Is she going to eat all of that?" A huge salad and creamy avocado and some nuts and a sprinkle of parmesan with grilled salmon or that big lamb burger? Yes, please. Sign me up.

STRATEGIES FOR THE WEEK

THE SIMPLY REAL HEALTH COOKBOOK | *Easy real food recipes for a healthy life, made simple.*

I often get asked how I plan out my week, food-wise. I'm a busy entrepreneur, and because I'm often in a time crunch, I need my food to be as efficient as possible. I also want to eat well. These are not mutually exclusive things in my world. So, my weekly shopping and prep goes a little something like this:

◇ I always have some kind of leafy greens on hand, for a green smoothie, for a salad, soup, or to be quickly sautéed with garlic, olive oil, salt and pepper.

◇ An avocado or two, for the same reason as above. It's a perfect addition to the greens however they are prepared, or just as a simple snack with sea salt and pepper or cumin sprinkled on top.

◇ One other veggie to roast, depending on what is in season and on sale, usually. It could be beets, asparagus, green beans, peppers, or tomatoes.

◇ Some hummus or healthy dip that will go with anything and that I can also use as a salad dressing.

◇ If it's warm out, I get some extra veggies to eat raw throughout the week, or cook into dishes. Tomatoes and peppers are two of my favorites because of their versatility.

◇ If it's cold out, I throw an onion, a carrot, and a few stalks of celery into my cart to make a soup base. Any extra veggies I get can also go into the soup, or in an easy stir fry with an amazing homemade dressing or sauce.

◇ A really good hard cheese like parmesan, pecorino or raw cheddar.

◇ An assortment of olives and pickled peppers to snack on or add to dishes.

◇ Some grass-fed meat, or wild fish. Something that cooks quickly, or I can make in a bigger batch and use in lots of ways, like **Easy Shredded Chicken** (see recipe) or organic ground turkey.

◇ Medjool dates. Always medjool dates, kept in the fridge for when I want something sweet.

On Better Shopping:

Rule #1: Don't buy anything you don't have a plan for. Seriously. Before you go shopping, look at your week. Don't be hopeful about "maybe" meals you'll eat at home. Be realistic. Know yourself. Know your schedule. Don't buy ingredients for longer recipes when you come home too starving to even think straight. And don't buy any produce without a plan for exactly how you're going to use it.

Make a list. Or just buy some multi-purpose ingredients like I do and get a little creative.

On Entertaining:

Light lots and lots of candles. Turn down overhead lights or string up some fun ones—you'd be amazed at how much this can change the mood, no matter the size of your dining room. Play music. Ambiance and how you make people feel are the keys here.

Have a signature cocktail or chilled bottle of wine ready when people come over. Let them be in the kitchen with you, and give them tasks. Use paper plates or fun paper napkins, or white cloth ones you can bleach—whatever works for your lifestyle. But here's the real big one—always, always have most of the food preparation done when people come over. Make two dishes at most, plus a great appetizer, and have your guests bring the rest.

Most of all, relax and enjoy the good company and time around the table. The best parties are never the ones where the host is stressed and striving for perfection. And, the dirty dishes can always wait.

FACT: traditional breakfast food is the worst way to start your day. They are usually heavy, processed grain and sugar dominant options that actually take more energy to digest than they give back to you. Plus, those grain-filled foods can make you a lot hungrier, sooner in your day. This is why I love green smoothies. They are packed with phytonutrients and enzymes to energize you, are light on your digestive system, and are so satisfying when you make them right. Plus on those busy mornings, you can pour them into a mason jar and drink them on the go. If you are just getting started in your new healthy lifestyle, swap out one of your meals for any one of these smoothies and take note of how your body feels in the hours that follow.

BREAKFAST + ANYTIME GREEN

SMOOTHIES

Sarah's Everyday Green Smoothie 28

Peanut Butter Date Green Smoothie 30

Cherry Green Smoothie 32

Sarah's Basic Kale Smoothie 34

Honeydew Mint Green Smoothie 36

Cinnamon Green Smoothie 38

Tropical Green Smoothie 40

SARAH'S EVERYDAY GREEN SMOOTHIE

- 1 cup frozen blueberries
- 1/2 avocado
- 1/2 banana
- 3 large handfuls of spinach (or more)
- 1 cup water
- 1 cup ice

MAKES ABOUT 1 SERVING

DIRECTIONS

Add banana, spinach, blueberries, avocado, and water to a blender. Blend first, then add ice and continue to blend until smooth.

This recipe is the best way to start making green smoothies! The first couple times you make this, use a small amount of spinach, then add more as you grow accustomed to it. When blended, this smoothie has a fresh, sweet taste.

PEANUT BUTTER + DATE GREEN SMOOTHIE

5	leaves romaine, butter lettuce, kale or 2 handfuls spinach		1	teaspoon peanut or almond butter
1/2	banana		1/2	cup water
1/2	avocado (optional)		1/2	cup coconut water
3	dried dates, pits removed		1	cup ice

MAKES ABOUT

1

SERVING

DIRECTIONS

Add greens, nut butter, dates, banana, avocado, coconut water, and water to a blender. Blend first, then add ice, and continue to blend until smooth.

To die for! This is a great beginner green smoothie recipe for kids and adults alike. For a fun twist, try adding 1-2 teaspoons of unsweetened cocoa powder for a chocolate peanut butter green smoothie.

CHERRY GREEN SMOOTHIE

MAKES ABOUT

1

SERVING

3-4 leaves of romaine lettuce or kale or 1 handful spinach
1/2 banana
1/3 cup frozen cherries (approximately 6 pieces)
1/2 cup water
1/4 cup coconut water
1 cup ice

Also try adding 1-2 teaspoons of unsweetened cocoa powder to make a chocolate cherry green smoothie. If it's not sweet enough to your liking, add ½ teaspoon of vanilla extract.

DIRECTIONS

Add greens, banana, cherries, coconut water, and water to the blender. Blend first, then add ice, and continue to blend until smooth.

SMOOTHIES

SMOOTHIES

SARAH'S BASIC KALE SMOOTHIE

3	stalks green kale, stems discarded
1/2	banana
1/2	avocado
1/3	cup frozen cherries or mangoes (approximately 6 pieces)
1	teaspoon chia seeds (optional)
1/4	cup coconut water (optional)
1/4	cup water
1/2	cup ice

MAKES ABOUT

1

SERVING

DIRECTIONS

Add kale, banana, avocado, frozen fruit, chia seeds, coconut water, and water to the blender. Blend first, then add ice, and continue to blend until smooth.

Ready for more leafy greens in your life? This recipe is a great way to start adding kale to your smoothies without it being too overpowering. Try this version with both frozen cherries or frozen mangos and see which one you like best.

HONEYDEW MINT GREEN SMOOTHIE

MAKES ABOUT

1

SERVING

5	leaves romaine lettuce or 2 handfuls of spinach	1/2	banana
1	handful chopped honeydew or cantaloupe (approximately ¼ cup to ½ cup)	5	leaves fresh mint
		1/2	cup coconut water
		1/4	cup water
		1	cup ice

DIRECTIONS

Add lettuce, melon, banana, mint, coconut water, and water to a blender. Blend first, then add ice, and continue to blend until smooth.

Other great additions or substitutions to this recipe could include coconut milk or avocado instead of banana; basil instead of mint; or peaches instead of honeydew. All of which are amazing.

CINNAMON GREEN SMOOTHIE

MAKES ABOUT 1 SERVING

- 1 cucumber, peeled
- 1 cup spinach
- 2 stalks green kale, stems discarded
- 1/2 banana
- 1/2 avocado
- 1 teaspoon vanilla extract
- 1 teaspoon cinnamon
- 1/2 cup water
- 1 cup ice

If you are ready for a refreshing and bright tasting smoothie, give this one a whirl. The cinnamon and cucumber are a great combination.

DIRECTIONS

Add cucumber, spinach, kale, banana, avocado, vanilla, cinnamon, and water to a blender. Blend first, then add ice, and continue to blend until smooth.

SMOOTHIES

TROPICAL GREEN SMOOTHIE

3	leaves romaine	1/2	cup coconut water
1/2	banana	1/2	cup water
1/4	cup frozen mango	1	cup ice
1/4	cup frozen pineapple		

MAKES ABOUT

1

SERVING

DIRECTIONS

Add romaine, banana, mango, pineapple, coconut water, and water to the blender. Blend first, then add ice, and continue to blend until smooth.

Bring a little tropical vacation into your morning routine with this recipe. This smoothie is also great with the addition of cinnamon, coconut meat, fresh papaya or lime.

OTHER BREAKFAST

+ BRUNCH IDEAS

Two Ingredient Pancakes **44**

Zucchini + Egg Muffins **46**

Balsamic Broiled Citrus **48**

Pumpkin Chocolate Granola **50**

Apple Cinnamon Morning Quinoa **52**

Flourless Carrot Cake Muffins **54**

Egg Potato Veggie Bake **56**

Vanilla Chia Seed Pudding **58**

Toasted Mochi with Peanut Butter + Honey **60**

Healthy Banana Bread **62**

Peaches + Cream on Steel-Cut Oats or Morning Quinoa **64**

TWO INGREDIENT PANCAKES

MAKES ABOUT

8

MEDIUM PANCAKES

AND

4

SERVINGS WHIPPED CREAM

These almost-too-simple and healthy pancakes are great served with natural peanut or almond butter, homemade whipped cream, Coconut Whipped Cream, berries, sliced bananas, seasonal fruit, or a drizzle of maple syrup or raw honey.

PANCAKES

- 1 large ripe banana
- 2 organic cage-free eggs
- 1/4 teaspoon baking powder
- 1/4 teaspoon cinnamon

COCONUT WHIPPED CREAM

- 1 can regular coconut milk
- 2 teaspoons vanilla extract

DIRECTIONS

Add all ingredients to a blender and blend until smooth. Or, mash banana by hand, then add eggs, baking powder and cinnamon to a bowl and mix well. Transfer mixture to a measuring cup with a spout for easy pouring.

Heat a bit of butter or coconut oil on a griddle or cast iron skillet on medium-high heat. Once warm, pour batter as you would with normal pancakes, flipping halfway when slightly browned, approximately 4 minutes on each side.

- Coconut Whipped Cream -

Serve this chilled sweet topping on its own, with fresh berries or other seasonal fruit, on top of the **Apple Cinnamon Morning Quinoa**, or the **Two Ingredient Pancakes**. Divine over chocolate desserts and the **Seasonal Fruit Crumble** too! Use regular coconut milk in this recipe, not the light version.

Place a can of coconut milk upside down in the fridge for 2 hours. When ready to prepare, flip the can right side up and open, scooping only the thick part of the mixture into a blender. Leave the coconut water behind (and use it in other smoothies, coffee, or iced tea). Add 2 teaspoons vanilla to the blender, and blend on low speed for 1 minute or until fluffy in texture.

OTHER BREAKFAST + BRUNCH IDEAS

OTHER BREAKFAST + BRUNCH IDEAS

ZUCCHINI + EGG MUFFINS

- **10** organic cage-free eggs
- **1** zucchini, grated or shredded with excess moisture squeezed out (use a paper towel)
- **1/2** onion, finely chopped
- **1/4** cup goat cheese, grated parmesan, or other artisan cheese of your choice (optional)
- **1** tablespoon fresh chopped herbs (chives, basil, or parsley)
- **+** sea salt and pepper to taste

MAKES ABOUT

12

MUFFINS

DIRECTIONS

Preheat oven to 400°F. Line a muffin tin with baking cups or grease the pan with butter or coconut oil. In a bowl, whisk eggs, zucchini, onion, herbs, and cheese with sea salt and pepper. Pour the batter into muffin tins and bake until cooked through (or not runny in the middle) for approximately 20 minutes. Broil for the last minute to get a nice brown crust.

These muffins are a great healthy breakfast for mornings on-the-go, and can easily be made ahead of time. Extra ingredients like chopped organic turkey or bacon, grated or chopped vegetables, or hot sauce can be great additions.

BALSAMIC BROILED CITRUS

MAKES ABOUT 4 SERVINGS

- 1 grapefruit, sliced in half
- 1 orange, sliced in half
- 2 teaspoons balsamic vinegar
- 2 teaspoons honey

DIRECTIONS

Set oven to broil. Add vinegar and honey to a small saucepan over low heat. Whisk to combine. Place grapefruit and orange halves skin-side down on a parchment-lined baking sheet, and drizzle with the warmed vinegar and honey mixture. Broil until browned and bubbly on top, about 1-2 minutes.

Talk about a stunning brunch idea. Try this recipe with limes and lemons for an even more colorful presentation! Fresh chopped basil or rosemary sprigs make an excellent garnish, as does a dollop of greek yogurt or crème fraiche, or a sprinkle of the **Pumpkin Chocolate Granola.**

OTHER BREAKFAST + BRUNCH IDEAS

PUMPKIN CHOCOLATE GRANOLA

MAKES ABOUT

SERVINGS

- 2 cups large coconut flakes
- 2 cups almonds, chopped
- 1 cup pumpkin seeds, shelled
- 1/4 cup organic maple syrup
- 2 tablespoons extra-virgin, unrefined coconut oil
- 1 1/2 tablespoons chia seeds
- 3 teaspoons cocoa powder
- 1/2 teaspoon cinnamon
- 1/2 teaspoon vanilla extract
- 1/2 teaspoon sea salt

DIRECTIONS

Preheat oven to 375°F. Line a baking sheet with parchment paper. In a saucepan over medium heat, melt coconut oil and maple syrup. Add cocoa powder, cinnamon, vanilla, and sea salt to the oil and syrup mixture, and stir well. Add the coconut flakes, almonds and pumpkin seeds to a larger prep bowl, and drizzle the coconut-maple mixture over the top. Toss well, and spread evenly on the baking sheet. Bake for 15 minutes or until crisp, stirring the mixture halfway through.

My all-time favorite morning (or any time of day) crunchy treat! It's delicious on its own, sprinkled over whole-milk greek yogurt, or as a cereal with whole milk. Once it cools, this granola keeps well in a sealed container in the fridge for up to 1 month.

OTHER BREAKFAST +
BRUNCH IDEAS

APPLE CINNAMON MORNING QUINOA

MAKES ABOUT

SERVINGS

1	cup dry quinoa
2	cups water
1	apple, core removed and chopped
1/4	teaspoon sea salt

TO ADD AFTER:

4	tablespoons coconut oil
2	teaspoons cinnamon
2	teaspoons chia seeds
1	handful raisins
+	sprinkle of slivered almonds

DIRECTIONS

Feel free to change up the fruit depending on the season. Other great additions include nutmeg, chopped nuts or dried fruit of your choice, coconut flakes, chopped dates, maple syrup or raw honey, peanut or almond butter, whole milk, or coconut milk.

Add 1 cup dry quinoa to a small saucepan with 2 cups water, sea salt, and chopped apple. Cover and bring to a boil. Once boiling, turn off heat, and let sit covered for 10-15 minutes until the quinoa is fluffy. Stir in coconut oil, cinnamon, chia seeds, raisins, and almonds, as well as any other toppings of your choice, and serve hot.

Make a big batch of this quinoa and freeze, or keep refrigerated in individual containers for easy warming during the week. Quinoa not only has more protein than steel cut oats, but also cooks much faster, which is why it is my favorite grain.

FLOURLESS CARROT CAKE MUFFINS

MAKES ABOUT **12** MUFFINS

- 3 cups shredded carrots
- 1 1/2 cups walnuts
- 2 tablespoons chia seeds (or 3 eggs)
- 1 1/2 teaspoons baking soda
- 1 teaspoon natural vanilla extract
- 2 teaspoons cinnamon
- 1/2 teaspoon garam masala (or nutmeg)
- 1/2 teaspoon cumin
- 1/2 cup unbleached sugar
- + zest of 1 lemon
- + pinch of sea salt

DIRECTIONS

These muffins are totally grain free, dairy free and egg free, making them a perfect pastry option for those that have food sensitivities or prefer a lighter meal in the morning.

Preheat oven to 375°F. Line muffin tins with unbleached baking cups or spray with coconut or olive oil. If you are using chia seeds, add them to a small bowl with water and stir to combine. Let sit while you prepare everything else.

Pulse walnuts in a strong blender or food processor until they have a flour-like texture. Add to a large mixing bowl.

Pulse carrots in the blender or food processor, adding a tiny bit of water if needed. Add to the mixing bowl with the walnut flour. Add lemon zest, sugar, baking soda, vanilla, garam masala, cinnamon, cumin, and a sprinkle of sea salt to the bowl. Add the soaked chia seeds or 3 eggs to the mixture and stir well.

Add mixture to baking cups, filling halfway. Bake for 35-40 minutes, or until done to your liking.

OTHER BREAKFAST + BRUNCH IDEAS

These are amazing toasted or served warm with melted coconut oil, grass-fed butter, natural peanut butter, almond butter, or tahini. Chia seeds soaked in water are an easy egg replacement both here and in other recipes. Doing so will give you a little extra crunch too!

EGG POTATO VEGGIE BAKE

MAKES ABOUT

10

SERVINGS

- 12 organic, cage-free eggs
- 6 baby potatoes, cut into quarters
- 1 package sliced mushrooms (approximately 1 cup)
- 1 red bell pepper, chopped
- 1 head chard, kale, or spinach, chopped
- 1 onion, chopped
- 3 cloves garlic, chopped
- 1 cup chopped herbs of your choice (chives, tarragon, basil, or parsley)
- 1/2 cup whole-milk ricotta cheese or artisan cheese of your choice (optional)
- + sea salt and pepper to taste

DIRECTIONS

Preheat oven to 350°F. Bring 2 or 3 cups water to boil in a large stock pot. Add quartered potatoes and cover; cook for 10-12 minutes or until they are mostly softened. Sauté chopped garlic and onions in a large frying pan with a dollop of butter or olive oil over medium heat.

After a few minutes, add mushrooms to the same pan. Add chopped peppers a few minutes later. When veggies are mostly cooked through, sprinkle with sea salt and pepper. Set aside, but keep the heat going on the stovetop—you will be cooking the leafy greens in this same pan.

Drain potatoes and add them to the bottom of a greased rectangular 9" x 13" glass or ceramic baking dish. Add sautéed veggies over the potatoes. Now, sauté the greens in the same pan until wilted. Add to the baking dish as well.

Whisk eggs in a bowl with sea salt, pepper, and chopped herbs. Pour the egg mixture into the baking dish, spreading it around evenly. Dollop with ricotta cheese and bake for 25-30 minutes, depending on the depth of your pan. Remove from the oven when the middle is no longer gooey. Broil at the end for a nice brown crust.

This recipe can be assembled ahead of time and baked right before serving, making it an ideal dish for large groups. Serve hot or at room temperature for breakfast, brunch, lunch, or dinner. Other great additions to this recipe could include crumbled organic sausage, sweet potatoes, zucchini, leeks, tomatoes, hot sauce, or salsa.

OTHER BREAKFAST + BRUNCH IDEAS

VANILLA CHIA SEED PUDDING

MAKES ABOUT

SERVINGS
depending on the size of jar you choose

1	16 ounce can regular coconut milk
10	teaspoons chia seeds
2	teaspoons vanilla
6	teaspoons maple syrup

DIRECTIONS

This amazing recipe is perfect for dessert or a healthier morning sweet treat.

Combine all ingredients in a glass mason jar, or multiple small jars (as pictured). Stir briskly or shake well to combine. Place in the fridge for at least 2 hours before eating.

This recipe is best after 24 hours in the fridge, when the chia seeds have had time to expand and firm up. Feel free to add more maple syrup or honey if you like. Or, try some other great additions like cocoa powder, a splash of coffee, chopped dark chocolate, fruit, coconut flakes, or cinnamon.

TOASTED MOCHI
with PEANUT BUTTER + HONEY

MAKES ABOUT 4 SERVINGS

- 4 mochi cubes
- 3 teaspoons natural peanut butter, almond butter, tahini or sunflower seed butter
- 2 teaspoons raw honey or maple syrup

DIRECTIONS

Mochi is a traditional Japanese style brown rice product that puffs up beautifully when toasted in the oven.

Preheat oven to 400°F. Line a baking sheet with parchment paper. Place mochi cubes on the baking sheet and bake according to directions on the package, about 8-10 minutes. The mochi is done when it starts expanding up and out. Remove from heat, slice in half, and spread peanut butter and honey (or other toppings of your choice) on each side. Add a dash of cinnamon, and serve warm.

Although its texture and taste makes it seem like a decadent start to the day, mochi's ingredients are very simple. Find it in the refrigerated section of most health food stores, usually by the yogurt. I love the cinnamon-date version if you can find it. Unwrap the package when you get home, cut the mochi into squares, and store in a plastic bag in the freezer until you're ready to use.

OTHER BREAKFAST + BRUNCH IDEAS

HEALTHY BANANA BREAD

- 4 ripe bananas, mashed
- 2 eggs (or 2 teaspoons chia seeds mixed with 5 teaspoons water)
- 1 2/3 cup gluten free flour (or almond + coconut flour combined)
- 1/2 cup coconut oil, melted
- 1 cup sugar or ½ cup maple syrup
- 1 teaspoon vanilla extract
- 1 teaspoon baking soda
- 1 teaspoon cinnamon
- 1/2 cup chopped walnuts

MAKES 1 LOAF

DIRECTIONS

Preheat oven to 350°F. Grease a loaf pan with coconut oil or butter. If you are using chia seeds instead of eggs, add them to a small bowl with water and let them soak while you prepare the rest of the ingredients. Mix all other ingredients together in a large bowl and pour into the greased pan. Bake for 45 minutes to 1 hour until the center is cooked through. You can easily check this with a toothpick or knife inserted in the middle of the loaf.

This recipe is awesome with the addition of chopped walnuts, pistachios, macadamia nuts, or chocolate chips, depending on who you're feeding. A thick slice of this banana bread is also excellent toasted with nut butter, or butter and cinnamon.

OTHER BREAKFAST + BRUNCH IDEAS

PEACHES + CREAM
STEEL CUT OATS OR MORNING QUINOA

GF | DF | V

- 1 cup gluten free, steel-cut oats or quinoa
- 1 peach, chopped
- 4 tablespoons coconut oil
- 4 tablespoons coconut milk (or hemp, almond or whole milk)
- 4 teaspoons pure maple syrup or raw honey (optional)
- 2 teaspoons cinnamon

MAKES ABOUT 4 SERVINGS

DIRECTIONS

Substitute your favorite fruit as the seasons change. Other great toppings could include shredded coconut, chopped nuts, cinnamon, raisins, or chopped dates.

Add dry steel-cut oats or quinoa to 1 cup water in a saucepan with the peaches, or put the peaches aside if you'd like to keep them fresh and add them on top before serving (as pictured). Add a pinch of sea salt, cover with a lid, and bring to a boil. Once boiling, reduce heat and simmer with the lid on. If you're making steel-cut oats, let the pan simmer for 15 minutes on the stove until all the water is absorbed; if you're making quinoa, simmer for 5 minutes.

Once the grains finish cooking, stir in coconut oil, coconut milk, and maple syrup or honey and any other toppings you like. Serve warm with a sprinkle of cinnamon.

If you're an oatmeal lover, this recipe is a great one to double and keep in the fridge. You can even freeze it in individual portions for quick and easy defrosting.

Make Ahead DISHES

Photoshoot Salad **68**
Feta + Basil Lentil Salad **70**
Kale, Avocado + Roasted Squash Salad **72**
Easy Roasted Vegetables **74**
Italian Tuna Salad **76**
Sesame Snap Peas **78**
Shredded Kale + Lentil Salad with Snap Peas and Peanut Sauce **80**
Spinach Quinoa Bake **82**
Roasted Apple, Fennel + Yam Salad **84**
Spiced Black Bean + Sweet Potato Salad **86**

Cold Sesame Soba Noodle Salad **88**
Mint + White Bean Salad **90**
Italian-Style Egg Salad **92**
Cashew Pesto Kale Salad **94**
Chunky Chopped Greek Salad **96**
French Potato Salad **98**
Sarah's Fresh Corn Salad **100**
Crab + Grapefruit Stuffed Avocados **102**
Wild Rice Salad with Grapes **104**
Hummus Collard Wraps **106**
Lentil Yogurt Dip + Salad **108**

Make-ahead dishes are my favorite thing to prepare. They take up most of this book, and for good reason. They are amazing. Functional, in the sexiest possible way. They're efficient, and even taste better over time. Plus, they can be morphed and combined into multiple different dishes. I actually think they are a busy person's key to a healthier lifestyle. Make one, and see how many ways you can eat it—over greens, with cheese, with different herbs, a different vinegar, adding protein, over quinoa or brown rice, in tacos, with avocados, or with chopped nuts. It all WORKS. Hallelujah. Healthy eating just got simplified.

MAKE AHEAD DISHES

PHOTOSHOOT SALAD

SALAD:

- 2 cans garbanzo beans, rinsed and drained
- 1 English cucumber, peeled with the seeds scooped out with a spoon
- 1/2 pint baby tomatoes, halved, or 1 red bell pepper, cubed
- 10 leaves fresh basil, finely chopped
- 1 avocado, cubed
- 1/4 cup parmesan cheese (optional)

DRESSING:

- 1 lemon, juiced
- \+ drizzle of olive oil
- \+ sea salt and pepper to taste

MAKES ABOUT

6

SERVINGS

DIRECTIONS

I made this salad on accident during my first photo shoot for simplyrealhealth.com. I was so nervous. And multitasking. And was supposed to be cooking something for the camera while smiling and trying not to cut myself. This recipe is what entailed. After a long day, the photographer tasted it, and she just smiled at me, nodding in silence. I tasted it after, not really believing her. Since then, I always make it while I'm being photographed in the kitchen (yes, even the cover of this book is a rendition of it). It's got great color, requires no cooking and is so satisfying. It's a perfect recipe to eat on its own, over mixed greens, mixed into cooked brown rice or quinoa, or over grilled meat or vegetables.

Combine all ingredients in a large bowl, except the avocado and parmesan. Add dressing and gently stir. Add avocado and parmesan when ready to serve. Garnish with extra chopped basil.

FETA + LENTIL BASIL SALAD

MAKES ABOUT

4

SERVINGS

- **2** cans lentils or 2 cups cooked french lentils
- **1** cup baby tomatoes, halved
- **1** avocado, cubed
- **10** leaves fresh basil, finely chopped
- **2** tablespoons red or white wine vinegar
- **+** sprinkle of feta cheese (optional)
- **+** sea salt and pepper to taste

This is one of my favorite hearty, make ahead salads anytime of the year. If you like cheese, I recommend using crumbled feta in this recipe—it's the perfect salty complement. Other vegetables make great additions as well: try cubed zucchini, carrots, celery, radishes or fennel.

DIRECTIONS

Serve this salad on its own, over salad greens, mixed with quinoa or brown rice, or as a party dip with organic corn chips.

Combine all ingredients, except the red wine vinegar and feta cheese, in a large bowl. Add vinegar and toss gently. Sprinkle with feta and garnish with extra basil to serve.

MAKE AHEAD DISHES

KALE, AVOCADO + ROASTED SQUASH SALAD

with MAPLE BASIL DRESSING

GF DF V MA

MAKES ABOUT

4

SERVINGS OF BOTH

SALAD:

- 2 heads leafy green kale
- 1 cup roasted butternut squash cubes (see **Roasted Vegetable** recipe for a basic how-to)
- 1 avocado, cubed
- 1/3 cup **Maple Basil Dressing**
- + sprinkle of crumbled feta cheese (optional)

MAPLE BASIL DRESSING:

- 1/4 cup olive oil
- 5 tablespoons red or white wine vinegar
- 2 tablespoons Dijon mustard
- 1 tablespoon maple syrup
- 10 fresh basil leaves
- 1/4 teaspoon sea salt
- 1/2 teaspoon pepper

DIRECTIONS

Think you don't like kale salad? Try this first. Marinating kale in dressing helps break down the kale's bitterness, and creates an excellent base for all kinds of meals, and makes it easy to take with you on the go.

Wash the kale, discard the stems, and tear the leaves into bite-sized pieces. Place in a large bowl. Dry leaves with a paper towel. Pour **Maple Basil Dressing** over the top and use your hands to massage it into the leaves. Add cooked squash and feta cheese. Add avocado right before serving.

- Maple Basil Dressing -

Store this in a small glass bottle or jar, and keep it in the fridge for up to 7 days.

Combine all ingredients in a blender and blend until smooth.

To add more substance to your salad, add baby tomatoes, cucumber slices, hard-boiled eggs, organic turkey or chicken, or some sesame or pumpkin seeds. To save time, use pre-cut frozen butternut squash cubes. This salad gets better with time—make a batch and keep it in the fridge for up to 3 days.

MAKE AHEAD DISHES

EASY ROASTED VEGETABLES

- **4** assorted vegetables of your choice: bell peppers, green beans, cauliflower, asparagus, broccoli, eggplant, zucchini, or whatever is in season
- **+** drizzle of extra-virgin olive oil
- **+** sprinkle of sea salt + pepper

MAKES ABOUT

4

SERVINGS

DIRECTIONS

These are delicious served hot or cold, on their own, on top of salads, or even puréed with broth to make a soup. Plus, they keep well in the fridge for up to 5 days.

Pre-heat oven to 400°F. Line a baking sheet with parchment paper. Cut veggies into pieces of approximately the same size (1 inch squares usually work well). Spread on a baking sheet, drizzle with olive oil and add sea salt and pepper. Hand-toss to coat vegetables. Place in the oven, and roast for 20-25 minutes or until the veggies start to brown on all sides.

Unlike steaming or frying, roasting brings out a vegetable's natural sugars, making them taste amazing to almost any palate. And it's so easy to do at home! All you need is a hot oven, olive oil, sea salt, and pepper.

MAKE AHEAD DISHES

ITALIAN TUNA SALAD

MAKES ABOUT

2

SERVINGS

- 2 cans wild-caught tuna, packed in water
- 4 celery stalks, or 1/2 cucumber or fennel bulb, finely chopped
- 1/2 pint baby tomatoes, quartered or halved
- 2 tablespoons extra-virgin olive oil
- 1 tablespoon dijon mustard
- \+ sea salt and pepper to taste

DIRECTIONS

This is a great basic recipe that you can dress up however you'd like—pickles, fennel, herbs, fresh or roasted bell peppers, sundried tomatoes, olives, red or green onions, or pesto would all be great additions here.

Combine tuna, olive oil, mustard, sea salt, and pepper in a bowl, and mix with a fork. Add tomatoes and celery (or other additions of your choice) and gently mix. Add more olive oil and mustard if desired.

Serve on its own, in a scooped-out tomato, on an avocado half, stuffed in mini peppers, or on top of mixed greens, a brown rice cake, toasted millet or sprouted grain bread. Keeps well in the fridge for up to 3 days.

SESAME SNAP PEAS

MAKES ABOUT
2
SERVINGS

1 cup snap peas, ends removed
1 tablespoon toasted sesame oil
2 or 3 teaspoons sesame seeds
+ sprinkle of sea salt

DIRECTIONS

Toss all ingredients together in a bowl.

This is the quickest and easiest make-ahead dish. A kid favorite too! Keeps well in the fridge for up to 3 days.

MAKE AHEAD DISHES

SHREDDED KALE + LENTIL SALAD
with SNAP PEAS + PEANUT SAUCE

MAKES ABOUT

2

SERVINGS SALAD

AND

8

SERVINGS PEANUT SAUCE

SALAD

- **1** head kale, stems removed and leaves chopped
- **1/2** can lentils, rinsed and drained (or 1/2 cup cooked lentils)
- **1** small handful snap peas, ends removed

PEANUT SAUCE

- **16** ounces canned coconut milk
- **5** tablespoons natural peanut butter, almond butter, or tahini
- **2** tablespoons tamari sauce (gf) or shoyu sauce
- **2** tablespoons honey
- **+** sprinkle of cayenne pepper + sea salt

DIRECTIONS

Combine kale, lentils and snap peas together in a bowl. Drizzle warm or cold peanut sauce over the salad and toss before serving.

- Peanut Sauce -

Use tamari sauce to keep this recipe gluten free.

Make the peanut sauce first by whisking all ingredients together in a saucepan over low heat for 3-5 minutes or until the peanut butter melts.

This dish is great served hot or cold, for lunch or dinner. Top with a fried egg for a quick and tasty breakfast. Other veggies, cooked meat, seafood, quinoa, or brown rice are also welcome additions. Crumbled goat or feta cheese and cilantro are excellent garnishes.

SPINACH QUINOA BAKE

MAKES ABOUT

SERVINGS

- 1 cup quinoa, dry
- 1 red bell pepper or 1 cup baby tomatoes, chopped
- 1 pound fresh spinach or kale (approximately 4 cups)
- 1 cup whole milk greek yogurt
- 2 eggs
- 1/2 onion, diced
- 2 cloves garlic, diced
- 1/2 teaspoon chili powder
- 1 tablespoon basil, thyme, or Italian seasoning
- + sea salt and pepper to taste

DIRECTIONS

Preheat oven to 350°F. Add uncooked quinoa to a small saucepan with 2 cups organic chicken or vegetable broth or water. Cover with lid, and bring to a boil. Once boiling, season generously with sea salt and pepper, turn off heat, and let sit covered for 10 minutes or until the quinoa is fluffy.

In a large skillet, sauté onion and garlic for 2-3 minutes. Add red pepper, chili powder and the Italian spices, and cook until softened, around 3-4 minutes. Add spinach, and sauté until wilted. Remove from heat. In a large bowl, add yogurt and eggs; whisk together. Add the quinoa and veggie mixture, and stir until combined. Pour mixture into a greased pie pan, and bake for 60 minutes. Broil for 3-4 minutes at the end for a nice brown color on top.

MAKE AHEAD DISHES

This is an amazing make-ahead dish for any time of day. It's also great with a green salad or other added veggies of your choice.

This is such a great side dish, especially in the fall and winter months! Optional to add raisins, white or garbanzo beans, lentils, curry powder, or cinnamon depending on your tastes. Perfect served on its own, scrambled with eggs and potatoes for a breakfast hash, over a green salad, or mixed into cooked quinoa or wild rice.

MAKE AHEAD DISHES

ROASTED APPLE, FENNEL + YAM SALAD

- 2 apples (any sweet variety), cut into ½ inch cubes
- 2 fennel bulbs, feathery fronds removed and bulb sliced
- 2 small to medium yams, cut into cubes
- 1 squash of your choice cubed (about 1 cup)
- 1/2 onion, thinly sliced

MAKES ABOUT
4
SERVINGS

DIRECTIONS

Preheat oven to 425°F. Line a baking sheet with parchment paper. Add apple, fennel, yam, squash, and onion pieces to the sheet. Drizzle with olive oil, and sprinkle with sea salt and pepper. Toss with your hands to coat, and roast for 30 minutes or until slightly browned on all sides.

SPICED BLACK BEAN + SWEET POTATO SALAD

MAKES ABOUT

SERVINGS

SALAD

- **1** large or 2 small sweet potatoes or yams, cubed
- **1** can black beans, rinsed and drained or 1 cup cooked black beans
- **1/4** cup cilantro or parsley leaves, chopped
- **1/4** cup slivered almonds

DRESSING

- **1** lime, juiced
- **1/2** orange, juiced
- **1** teaspoon red wine vinegar
- **1/2** teaspoon cumin
- **1/4** teaspoon sea salt
- **1/4** teaspoon pepper

DIRECTIONS

Preheat oven to 400°F. Add sweet potato cubes to a parchment-lined baking sheet. Drizzle with olive oil and roast for 20-25 minutes until cooked through. In the meantime, add black beans, chopped herbs, and almonds to a bowl. Whisk dressing ingredients together in a small bowl. After the sweet potato cools, add it to the bean and herb mixture, and gently toss with the dressing to serve.

This is a great side dish on its own, used as a taco filling, combined with brown rice or quinoa, or as a chunky tapenade over fish, chicken, pork, or steak. Optional to add some Hungarian paprika, smoked paprika, or cayenne pepper for more spice. Avocado, toasted pumpkin seeds, or a sprinkle of feta or goat cheese make great additions as well.

COLD SESAME SOBA NOODLE SALAD

MAKES ABOUT

2

SERVINGS

SALAD

- **4-6** ounces buckwheat soba or rice noodles
- **1/2** cucumber, peeled and sliced into rounds
- **1/2** carrot, sliced, chopped, or shredded
- **3** radishes, thinly sliced
- **1** tablespoon sesame seeds
- **2** green onions, chopped (optional)
- **1** handful chopped basil (optional)

DRESSING

- **1** tablespoon toasted sesame oil
- **1** tablespoon rice-wine vinegar
- **1** lime, juiced
- **1/2** teaspoon sea salt

DIRECTIONS

Look for 100% buckwheat or rice noodles to keep this recipe gluten free.

Cook noodles according to the package directions. Rinse and drain. Whisk dressing in a separate bowl, and pour over the noodles. Add veggies, and sprinkle with more sesame seeds, chopped basil, and green onions to garnish.

MAKE AHEAD DISHES

Optional to add seafood, meat, or avocado. Keeps well, once dressed, in the fridge for up to 3 days.

MINT + WHITE BEAN SALAD

MAKES ABOUT

SERVINGS

2	cans white or cannellini beans, rinsed and drained
2	English cucumbers, peeled, seeds scooped out, then cubed
2	yellow or red bell peppers, cubed
8	fresh mint leaves, chopped
1	lemon, juiced
+	sea salt and pepper to taste

Cannellini beans can also be called white beans, white navy beans, or great northern beans at the store. This salad is great on its own or over greens of your choice. Optional additions include organic feta cheese, green or sweet onions, or wild tuna or grilled chicken.

DIRECTIONS

Combine beans, cucumbers, peppers and mint in a bowl and gently toss with lemon juice, sea salt, and pepper.

MAKE AHEAD DISHES

ITALIAN-STYLE EGG SALAD

MAKES ABOUT 4 SERVINGS

- 6 organic cage-free eggs
- 2 celery stalks, chopped
- 2 tablespoons chopped pickles, artichoke hearts, or roasted red peppers (or all three) (optional)
- 2 tablespoons dijon mustard
- 1 teaspoon pepper
- 1/2 teaspoon sea salt

DIRECTIONS

Bring a few cups of water to a boil over the stove (enough to cover the eggs). When boiling, gently add eggs to the water, and cook for 8 minutes. Remove and let cool or run under cold water before peeling. Combine all ingredients and mash well with a fork. Add a bit of olive oil if the mixture is dry. Adjust seasonings as necessary.

This mayonnaise-free egg salad recipe is great on a toasted baguette, or toasted sprouted grain or millet bread. Also great in a scooped-out tomato, bell pepper, or avocado. Stays fresh for 2 days in the fridge.

This salad is amazing on its own, or as a base for other veggies, nuts, seeds, meat, or seafood of your choice. Rubbing the olive oil and sauce into the kale leaves helps break down the kale's bitterness, so even if you think you don't like kale, try this first—it has converted masses. Tastes best after 24 hours in the fridge.

CASHEW PESTO KALE SALAD

- 1 1/2 heads leafy green kale (not Italian/Lacinato/Dinosaur kale)
- 3/4 cup raw cashews
- 1 1/2 ounces fresh basil leaves, stems removed
- 3 tablespoons nutritional yeast
- 1 lemon, juiced
- 1/2 teaspoon sea salt
- 1/2 teaspoon pepper
- + drizzle of olive oil

MAKES ABOUT

4

SERVINGS

DIRECTIONS

This is my absolute favorite recipe of everything I have ever created in my kitchen. It's a must try! Not only does it keep well for up to 4 days in the fridge, it's hearty and filling too. Using nutritional yeast keeps this pesto recipe dairy free and adds great flavor with some extra B vitamins to boot.

Combine all ingredients except kale in a blender with a small amount of water. Wash kale well and discard the stems. Tear kale into bite-sized pieces and place in a large bowl. Dry leaves with a paper towel or clean dish towel. Drizzle with olive oil and rub it into the leaves with your hands. Add the pesto and continue to do the same, trying to coat as many of the kale's crevices as you can. Best when served cold.

CHUNKY CHOPPED GREEK SALAD

SALAD

- 2 large cucumbers
- 2 bell peppers
- 12 pitted Kalamata olives, sliced in half
- 1/2 red onion, finely chopped
- 2 teaspoons dried oregano, basil, or dill (or 4 teaspoons fresh)

DRESSING

- 1/2 lemon, juiced
- \+ drizzle of olive oil
- \+ sea salt and pepper to taste

MAKES ABOUT

SERVINGS

DIRECTIONS

Peel cucumbers, remove ends, and slice each in half, lengthwise down the middle. Use a spoon to scoop out and discard the inner seeds. Slice cucumber into strips, then into small cubes, and add to a mixing bowl. Cut peppers and onion into similar sized cubes and add to the bowl, including the olives and herbs. Drizzle all ingredients with dressing and toss gently before serving.

This dish tastes best after a day marinating in the fridge! Great additions include crumbled feta cheese and fresh chopped mint. This makes a perfect side dish or chunky salsa to add over grilled seafood, green salads, or meat.

FRENCH POTATO SALAD

MAKES ABOUT 6 SERVINGS

SALAD

- **1** pound baby potatoes, any variety (approximately 12 potatoes)

DRESSING

- **1/2** cup olive oil
- **1/2** cup chopped fresh basil, dill, and parsley (or any combination of fresh herbs)
- **1/4** cup white wine vinegar or apple cider vinegar
- **3** tablespoons dijon mustard
- **1/4** teaspoon sea salt
- **1/4** teaspoon pepper

DIRECTIONS

Cut potatoes into quarter sized chunks. Boil for 10-15 minutes or until easily poked with a fork. Drain potatoes, rinse with cold water, and set aside in a large bowl.

Whisk ingredients for the dressing together and pour over the top of the cooled potatoes. Toss together gently and season with extra sea salt and pepper to taste.

This is a light vinaigrette-style potato salad, made in the traditional French style. It makes a perfect picnic salad or side dish. Other great additions include chopped celery, artichoke hearts, roasted red peppers, sweet onions, pickles, relish, or grilled chicken. Keeps well in the fridge for 3-4 days.

SARAH'S FRESH CORN SALAD

MAKES ABOUT

6

SERVINGS

SALAD

- 2 ears organic corn, kernels sliced off the cob, or 1 can rinsed and drained
- 2 red bell peppers, cubed
- 1/2 cup chopped cilantro leaves
- 1 avocado, cubed

DRESSING

- 2 tablespoons olive oil
- 2 limes, juiced
- 1 tablespoon red wine vinegar
- + sprinkle of cumin
- + sea salt and pepper to taste

A perfect side dish, dipping salsa, taco filling, or tapenade for grilled seafood or meat. Add the avocado right before serving. Smoked paprika or chipotle chili powder are optional, but highly recommended.

DIRECTIONS

Whisk dressing ingredients together or shake in a glass mason jar. Gently toss all ingredients (except avocado) and dressing together in a bowl to combine. Add avocado right before serving.

MAKE AHEAD DISHES

CRAB + GRAPEFRUIT STUFFED AVOCADOS

- **4** avocados, cut in half and rubbed with lime juice right before serving
- **1/2** pound cooked Dungeness crab meat (or baby shrimp)
- **1** cucumber, peeled, seeds scooped out and cubed
- **1** red bell pepper, cubed
- **1** grapefruit, peeled with membrane removed and cubed
- **1/2** red onion, very thinly sliced, then chopped
- **1/2** cup cilantro leaves, chopped
- **2** limes, juiced
- **1** teaspoon pepper
- **1/2** teaspoon sea salt

MAKES ABOUT

SERVINGS

DIRECTIONS

Add all ingredients together, except the avocados, in a large mixing bowl and stir the mixture to combine. Scoop into avocado halves right before you are ready to serve.

This crab salad is perfect on its own, over mixed greens, or served as ceviche with organic corn chips. My favorite version is served in avocado halves (as pictured) for a dish that is as beautiful as it is delicious.

WILD RICE SALAD
with GRAPES

MAKES ABOUT 4 SERVINGS

- **2** cups wild or black rice
- **1** cup arugula
- **1/2** cup red grapes, halved
- **1/2** cup walnuts, chopped
- **1/4** cup or sprinkle of crumbled feta cheese

DIRECTIONS

Bring rice and 4 cups of water to a boil with ½ teaspoon of sea salt. Once boiling, cover and reduce heat to low for 30 minutes, or until all the water is absorbed. While rice is cooking, slice grapes and chop walnuts. Add arugula, grapes, walnuts, and feta to cooked rice and stir. Add pepper to taste and drizzle with olive oil before serving.

Try this recipe with black rice, millet, quinoa, or any cooked whole grain you have in your pantry. If you don't have grapes, try raisins, currants, beets, chopped apples or pears, depending on the season. You can easily swap out the walnuts for pistachios, almonds, or pumpkin seeds.

MAKE AHEAD DISHES

HUMMUS COLLARD WRAPS

MAKES ABOUT

SERVINGS

- 1 bunch of collard greens, washed with stems removed (slice where the leaf ends)
- 2 handfuls mixed greens or chopped romaine (optional)
- 1 red bell pepper, thinly sliced
- 2 cucumbers, seeds removed and thinly sliced into matchsticks with a knife or into ribbons with a vegetable peeler
- 2 avocados, sliced
- 1 container hummus
- 1 lemon, juiced

DIRECTIONS

Feel free to swap out ingredients as you see fit. There are no rules with the fillings; just leave enough room to roll them up!

Wash all ingredients. Slice the cucumber, pepper, and avocado and set up in an assembly line. Spread the collard green leaf out. Smear a big spoonful of hummus in the middle of the leaf, add your mixed greens or lettuce on top, then add the bell peppers, cucumbers, and avocado. Squeeze a bit of lemon juice over the top, and sprinkle with sea salt and pepper.

Roll the broad side of the collard green first, then tuck the shorter sides in before you roll the rest. Wrap it up like a burrito in foil or plastic wrap, and stick in the fridge, or use toothpicks to hold them together until you're ready to eat.

If you are worried about the taste of collard greens, just add a bit more hummus or avocado. Collard greens are the big, fan-like greens with white stems. Try to buy the ones with the biggest leaves for this recipe. These wraps stay fresh for up to 3 days in the fridge.

LENTIL + YOGURT DIP SALAD

- **1** cup whole milk greek yogurt
- **3** cups cooked lentils (canned, steamed, or tiny French dry lentils that you soak and cook yourself)
- **4** green onions, thinly chopped
- **1** tablespoon chopped chives (approximately 6 stems)
- **+** sea salt and pepper to taste

MAKES ABOUT

6

SERVINGS

DIRECTIONS

Combine all ingredients together. Adjust seasonings as necessary.

This is a great dip with veggies, chips, or crackers of your choice. Also excellent on top of salad greens for an easy and satisfying lunch.

My salads are not the meek, skimpy kind that leave you hungry and kind of cranky. These are meals. Big, sexy meals with substance and texture, and some amazing homemade dressings. These recipes are designed to make eating vegetables a lot more joyful and satisfying. So you'll want to do it more. So you'll start feeling better. See where I'm going with this? Wimpy salads, out. Awesome salads, in.

entrée
SALADS

Grilled Prawn + Artichoke Salad **112**

Falafel Salad **114**

Asian Chicken + Cabbage Salad **116**

Mango Chicken Salad **120**

Sundried Tomato + Pulled Chicken Salad **122**

Roasted Beet + Ricotta Salad **124**

House Mixed Greens with Apple Cider Vinaigrette **126**

The Cobb Wedge Salad **128**

Mediterranean Spinach Salad **130**

Chopped Italian Salad **132**

Shredded Chicken, Avocado + Kale Quinoa Salad **134**

Spanish Caprese Salad **136**

Cabbage Slaw Salad with Spicy Honey-Cilantro Dressing **138**

Kale or Romaine Caesar Salad, Grilled or Classic **140**

GRILLED PRAWN + ARTICHOKE SALAD

MAKES ABOUT

4

SERVINGS

1/2	pound wild prawns
1	can artichoke hearts, drained, rinsed, and chopped
1	bell pepper or 1 carton baby tomatoes, sliced
1	cucumber, peeled, seeds scooped out, and cubed
3	green onion stalks, finely chopped
1	handful parsley leaves, thinly sliced
1	lemon, juiced
+	sea salt and pepper to taste

If you don't like seafood, try adding shredded or grilled chicken, or steak instead, or skip it altogether—it'll still be delicious and flavorful. This salad is great on its own or served over chopped romaine lettuce, and will keep well in the fridge for a few days.

DIRECTIONS

Preheat a skillet or the grill to medium-high heat. Add prawns and cook, approximately 5 minutes, flipping halfway in between. Add the rest of the ingredients together in a large mixing bowl. Add prawns on top of the salad. Drizzle all with lemon juice and sprinkle with sea salt, pepper, and extra parsley to serve.

ENTRÉE SALADS

FALAFEL SALAD

SALAD

2	cups mixed greens or 2 heads romaine lettuce, chopped
6-8	baked **Mini Falafel Patties** (see recipe)
1/2	pint baby tomatoes, halved, or 1/2 red bell pepper, chopped
1/2	cucumber or 1/2 fennel bulb, sliced
1/2	avocado, cubed
+	sprinkle of crumbled feta cheese (optional)

MINI FALAFEL PATTIES

1	can garbanzo beans
1/2	onion, chopped
1	cup parsley leaves
1	cup cilantro leaves
3	teaspoons cumin
1	clove garlic
1	teaspoon chia seeds
+	sea salt and pepper to taste

MAKES ABOUT

2

SERVINGS SALAD
AND

16

MINI FALAFELS

DIRECTIONS

Add all salad ingredients together. Serve with a drizzle of lemon juice and olive oil or *Cucumber Yogurt Dressing* or *Green Goddess Dressing*.

- Mini Falafel Patties -

These are a great snack, or meal as a part of the Falafel Salad.

Preheat oven to 375°F. Line a baking sheet with parchment paper. Add all ingredients to a blender or food processor and blend together.

Scoop the falafel batter with a 1 tablespoon measuring spoon, and space evenly on the baking sheet, flattening just slightly on top with the back of the spoon.

Bake for 30 minutes, then flip and cook another 5 minutes until done and lightly browned.

This salad is great on its own, or added inside sprouted grain tortillas or pita bread for a tasty lunch on the go.

ENTRÉE SALADS

ASIAN CHICKEN + CABBAGE SALAD

MAKES ABOUT

4

SERVINGS

SALAD

- 1 head green cabbage, middle core removed and thinly sliced
- 1/2 cup shredded chicken (optional) (see **Easy Shredded Chicken** recipe)
- 2 medium carrots, shredded
- 4 green onions, thinly sliced
- 1/2 cup cilantro leaves, chopped
- 1/4 cup peanuts, chopped
- 1 teaspoon sesame seeds
- + **Cilantro Lime + Ginger Dressing** to taste

CILANTRO, LIME + GINGER DRESSING

- 1/4 cup fresh lime juice (approximately 4 limes)
- 1/2 cup olive oil
- 2 tablespoons tamari sauce
- 2 teaspoons chopped cilantro
- 1 teaspoon unrefined sesame oil
- 1 tablespoon greek yogurt (optional)
- 1 teaspoon fresh ginger
- 1 teaspoon honey

*To save time, you can use pre-shredded carrots and cabbage in this recipe. Great served with the **Cilantro Lime + Ginger Dressing** and **Easy Shredded Chicken** on top. Keeps well in the fridge for up to 2 days with dressing on it.*

DIRECTIONS

Add ingredients to a large bowl and toss with dressing. Garnish with extra peanuts, cilantro, and lime wedges if desired.

- Cilantro, Lime + Ginger Dressing -

Also great on grilled steak and seafood!

In a glass jar or bowl, whisk ingredients together, or blend together until smooth.

> THE GOAL? TO EAT VEGETABLES AT EVERY MEAL. IDEALLY. BUT IF THAT SEEMS OVERWHELMING, START WITH AT LEAST ONE MEAL AND WORK YOUR WAY UP. YOUR TASTEBUDS *WILL* START TO SHIFT.

MANGO CHICKEN SALAD

SALAD

- 2 heads romaine lettuce, or 4 cups spinach or mixed greens
- 1 cup organic shredded chicken (see **Easy Shredded Chicken** recipe)
- 1 mango, peeled, pitted and chopped
- 1/4 cup pistachios (or slivered almonds)
- + sprinkle goat or blue cheese crumbles to taste

DRESSING

- 1/4 cup olive oil
- 6 tablespoons balsamic vinegar
- 2 teaspoons dijon mustard
- 1/4 teaspoon sea salt
- 1/4 teaspoon pepper

MAKES ABOUT

2

SERVINGS

DIRECTIONS

Combine lettuce, chicken, pistachios, mango and goat cheese. Whisk dressing ingredients together in a separate container, and toss before serving.

Beautiful when garnished with fresh chopped basil or cilantro. If you can't find fresh mango at the store, try using papaya, pineapple, cherries, blueberries, apples, or pears.

SUNDRIED TOMATO + PULLED CHICKEN SALAD

MAKES ABOUT **4** SERVINGS

Without the dressing, this salad holds up nicely in the fridge for 2 days.

SALAD

- 2 heads romaine, chopped
- 1 organic chicken breast
- 1 cup sundried tomatoes, chopped
- 1/4 cup slivered almonds or pine nuts
- 1 tablespoon Herbs de Provence or Italian-mixed herbs
- + sprinkle of goat or feta cheese

DRESSING

- 8 tablespoons extra-virgin olive oil
- 4 tablespoons red-wine vinegar
- 2 tablespoons dijon mustard
- + sea salt and pepper to taste

DIRECTIONS

Fill a saucepan with approximately 2 cups of water and bring to a boil. Once boiling, add the chicken breast, and reduce heat to a simmer. Cover and let cook for approximately 15 minutes, or until the chicken can be easily pulled apart with a fork.

Wash and chop the romaine. Dry with a paper towel or salad spinner, and place in a large serving bowl. Sprinkle sundried tomatoes and nuts over the greens.

Drain chicken and let cool for a minute. Pull apart into bite-sized pieces with a fork or your hands. Add to a small bowl and drizzle with olive oil, sea salt, pepper, and Herbs de Provence. Toss to coat. Add feta, and toss with dressing to serve.

ENTRÉE SALADS

ROASTED BEET + RICOTTA SALAD

MAKES ABOUT

SERVINGS

- 1 large red beet, peeled and cubed
- 1 large golden beet, peeled and cubed
- 2 tablespoons whole milk ricotta cheese
- 4 cups arugula
- 1 lemon, juiced
- + sea salt and pepper to taste

DIRECTIONS

Preheat oven to 400°F and line a baking sheet with parchment paper. Peel beets with a sharp paring knife or vegetable peeler and cut into cubes. Add to the baking sheet, drizzle with olive oil, sea salt, and pepper, and toss well. Bake for 30-35 minutes or until you can easily poke through them with a fork. Remove from oven. Assemble salad greens and ricotta, and scatter roasted beets over the top. Squeeze with lemon juice before serving.

Using a combination of golden and red beets gives this salad great color. Choose the biggest beets you can find at the store—they are much easier to peel and cut than small ones. When you bring them home, always remove the beet greens immediately and store them separately in the fridge until you're ready to use them.

ENTRÉE SALADS

HOUSE MIXED GREENS
with APPLE CIDER VINAIGRETTE

MAKES ABOUT 2 SERVINGS

SALAD

- 2 cups mixed greens, spinach or butter lettuce
- + shredded parmesan or pecorino cheese

APPLE CIDER VINAIGRETTE

- 2 tablespoons extra-virgin olive oil
- 1 tablespoon raw apple cider vinegar
- 2 teaspoons dijon mustard
- + sprinkle of sea salt and pepper to taste

DIRECTIONS

- Apple Cider Vinaigrette -

Whisk all dressing ingredients together with a fork, or shake in a glass mason jar. Pour over greens and toss gently before serving.

Other great additions to this simple and tangy salad dressing: sliced apples or avocados, radishes, chopped nuts, grilled chicken or fish, or fresh herbs of your choice.

COBB WEDGE SALAD
with GREEN GODDESS DRESSING

MAKES ABOUT 4 SERVINGS

SALAD

- 1 head iceberg lettuce
- 1 roma tomato, seeds scooped out and chopped (or ½ pint baby tomatoes, halved)
- 1 cucumber, seeds scooped out and chopped
- 4 slices organic bacon or turkey bacon
- 2 hard-boiled eggs, cubed
- 1 avocado, cubed
- 1 handful crumbled blue cheese (or feta, goat, or parmesan cheese) (optional)

GREEN GODDESS DRESSING

- 1/2 avocado
- 5 tablespoons olive oil
- 10 leaves fresh basil
- 1 handful chives (approximately 6 stalks), chopped
- 1 lemon, juiced
- 1 teaspoon anchovy paste
- + sea salt and pepper to taste

DIRECTIONS

Fry bacon in coconut oil, olive oil, or butter and set aside to cool. Hard boil 2 eggs by adding them to a boiling pot of water for 8 minutes. Slice iceberg lettuce into four equal quarters and plate on each dish, adding the tomatoes, cucumber, avocado, bacon, hard boiled egg, and cheese on top. Whisk dressing ingredients together and drizzle over the top to serve.

- Green Goddess Dressing -

This is a great dressing for any salad, marinade for any meat or fish, or colorful dip for a crudité platter.

Blend all ingredients together in a blender or food processor. Add more olive oil if you prefer a thinner consistency. Store in the fridge for up to 6 days.

*Undressed and without the avocado and cheese added, this salad can keep fresh in the fridge for up to 2 days, making it a perfect lunch or make-ahead meal. The **Everyday Balsamic Dressing** or **Green Goddess Dressing** compliments this dish perfectly.*

MEDITERRANEAN SPINACH SALAD

MAKES ABOUT

4

SERVINGS

SALAD

- 8 cups organic spinach
- 1/4 cup pitted kalamata olives, halved
- 1/2 pint baby tomatoes, halved
- 1/2 cucumber, seeds scooped out and sliced
- 1 can garbanzo beans, rinsed and drained

BASIC BALSAMIC DRESSING

- 6 tablespoons extra virgin olive oil
- 2 tablespoons balsamic vinegar
- 4 teaspoons dijon mustard
- + sea salt and pepper to taste

DIRECTIONS

Layer spinach in a large bowl. Add olives, tomatoes, cucumbers, and garbanzo beans on top. Toss with dressing before serving.

- Basic Balsamic Dressing -

Whisk all dressing ingredients together in a bowl, or shake in a glass mason jar.

Excellent on its own or with organic crumbled goat cheese, feta cheese, grilled chicken, fish, or steak.

ENTRÉE SALADS

CHOPPED ITALIAN SALAD

MAKES ABOUT

4

LARGE SERVINGS

SALAD

- 2 heads of romaine lettuce, finely chopped
- 1 can garbanzo beans, rinsed and drained
- 1 cup baby tomatoes, halved
- 1 cucumber, peeled, seeds scooped out, and chopped
- 1 avocado, cubed
- 10 leaves fresh basil, snipped or chopped
- 5 slices of organic turkey, ham, or salami, or any combination of the three

DRESSING

- 4 tablespoons olive oil
- 2 tablespoons balsamic or red wine vinegar
- 1 tablespoon dijon mustard
- \+ sea salt and pepper to taste

DIRECTIONS

Chop romaine into bite sized pieces. Wash and pat dry with a towel or in a salad spinner. Rinse and drain garbanzo beans. Add beans, tomatoes, cucumber, and meat to the salad greens. Drizzle with the dressing and add avocado right before serving. Garnish with extra basil if desired.

Without the avocado and dressing, this can be made ahead of time and kept in the fridge for up to 3 days. Look for nitrate-free sliced turkey, ham, and salami if possible. Optional to add shredded mozzarella or parmesan before serving.

SHREDDED CHICKEN, AVOCADO + KALE QUINOA SALAD

MAKES ABOUT 4 SERVINGS

SALAD

- 2 cups cooked quinoa (see **Basic Quinoa** recipe)
- 1 organic chicken breast, cooked (see **Easy Shredded Chicken** recipe)
- 1 avocado, cubed
- 8 cups chopped kale, spinach, or arugula leaves.

DRESSING

- 4 tablespoons olive oil
- 2 tablespoons red or white wine vinegar
- 1 tablespoon dijon mustard
- + sea salt and pepper to taste

DIRECTIONS

Combine all ingredients in a bowl, and toss with dressing to serve.

This is a great recipe to add in any extra veggies of your choice! Asparagus, celery, jicama, tomatoes and diced peppers would all be welcome additions. Keeps well in the fridge for up to 2 days without the avocado.

This recipe is a great no-cook meal in the summer, or party appetizer any time of the year.

SPANISH CAPRESE SALAD

MAKES ABOUT 8 SERVINGS

- **6** medium heirloom tomatoes
- **1** handful baby tomatoes, halved (orange or yellow add great color)
- **8** ounces whole milk mozzarella, sliced into rounds, or 8 baby mozzarella balls sliced in half
- **1** handful Spanish green olives
- **1** handful fresh basil, finely chopped
- **+** extra virgin olive oil
- **+** sea salt and pepper to taste

DIRECTIONS

Layer heirloom tomato slices with mozzarella cheese rounds. Scatter baby tomatoes and olives over the top and sprinkle with chopped basil. Sprinkle with sea salt, pepper, and olive oil to serve.

Other fun additions and twists on the original recipe include different types of cheeses, chopped pistachios, capers, roasted red peppers, red pepper flakes, chopped garlic, balsamic vinegar, or chopped parsley. Serve on its own, with a crusty loaf of bread, or toasted sprouted grain or millet bread.

CABBAGE SLAW SALAD
with SPICY HONEY-CILANTRO DRESSING

SALAD

- 1 organic chicken breast or 4 thin-cut chicken tenders or 1 medium piece wild fish or 8 wild prawns
- 4 cups pre-cut cabbage slaw or ½ head green cabbage, finely chopped
- 1 bell pepper, any color, chopped
- 1 avocado, cubed
- 1 ear organic corn, kernels sliced off the cob
- 1 can pinto beans, rinsed and drained
- + chopped cilantro leaves to garnish

SPICY HONEY-CILANTRO DRESSING

- 4 tablespoons olive oil
- 2 tablespoons whole milk greek yogurt
- 3 teaspoons honey
- 2 teaspoons hot sauce (or more if you like spice)
- 1/2 cup cilantro leaves, chopped
- 1 large or 2 small limes, juiced
- + sea salt and pepper to taste

MAKES ABOUT

2

SERVINGS SALAD
AND

6

SERVINGS DRESSING

One of my very favorite salads—and very favorite ways to convert people to cabbage lovers. Great on its own or as a taco filling.

DIRECTIONS

Cook chicken, fish, or shrimp on the stovetop, or grill on the barbecue over high heat, flipping only when you get a good sear on the first side. Slice or keep whole to serve.

In the meantime, make dressing by combining all ingredients in the blender. Blend until smooth.

Add cabbage, pinto beans, corn, peppers, and avocado to a large bowl. Toss salad with dressing. Add grilled chicken, fish, or shrimp over the top and garnish with extra cilantro.

KALE OR ROMAINE CAESAR
GRILLED or CLASSIC

MAKES ABOUT 2 SERVINGS

FOR EITHER SALAD PREPARATION

- 2 hearts romaine lettuce, cut in half lengthwise or 2 bunches Italian/Lacinato kale, bottom stems removed

CAESAR DRESSING

- 1/2 lemon, juiced
- 4 tablespoons olive oil
- 1 teaspoon anchovy paste (or gluten free worcestershire sauce)
- 1 teaspoon dijon mustard
- 1 clove garlic, finely chopped
- \+ sea salt and pepper to taste

DIRECTIONS

- Caesar Dressing -

Whisk all dressing ingredients together in a bowl or shake in a glass mason jar.

- Traditional Caesar Salad -

Toss chopped romaine or kale with the dressing. Add black pepper, parmesan cheese, and red pepper flakes to serve.

- Grilled Caesar Salad -

Rub each flat side of the romaine lettuce with some olive oil (or lightly rub each leaf of the kale). Preheat the grill to medium-high and place lettuce with the inner core facing down for a few minutes until you get some good grill marks. Remove from heat and drizzle dressing over the top to serve.

Sprinkle with black pepper, grated parmesan cheese, and red pepper flakes to serve.

You can make this salad traditionally with romaine lettuce or switch it up and use kale. Or even try it grilled for an extra special touch and boost of flavor. Optional to serve with grilled chicken, steak, or wild prawns for an entrée style salad.

The original one-pot meal. Soups and stews are an easy way to get more vegetables in your life. Take these recipes and make them your own by adding other veggies, meat, beans, lentils, quinoa, brown rice, or extra spices. Try them pureed or chunky. Hot or cold. In a slow cooker or on the stovetop. You can't go wrong with so many healthy foods in one dish.

SIMPLE, HEARTY + DELICIOUS

SOUPS

Creamy Apple Butternut Squash Soup **144**

Tuscan White Bean Stew **146**

Poblano Quinoa Chicken Chili **148**

Split Pea + Carrot Soup **150**

Coconut Corn Chowder **152**

Watermelon-Cucumber Gazpacho **156**

Hearty Lentil Stew **158**

Mulligatawny Soup **160**

White Bean + Chicken Chili Verde **162**

Rustic Vegetable + Bean Chili **164**

Tomato-Basil Soup **166**

Moroccan Lamb or Veggie Stew **168**

Classic Chicken and Vegetable Soup **170**

CREAMY-APPLE BUTTERNUT SQUASH SOUP

MAKES ABOUT 6 SERVINGS

- 1 butternut squash, peeled and cubed (or 3 cups of pre-cut squash cubes)
- 1 medium granny smith apple, cubed
- 1/2 onion, chopped
- 2 cups organic chicken or vegetable broth
- 1/4 cup heavy cream, whole milk or coconut milk
- 1 tablespoon dried sage
- \+ sea salt and pepper to taste

DIRECTIONS

In a large soup pot over medium heat, add a bit of coconut or olive oil and squash cubes. Cover with lid. After 5 minutes, stir and add apple and onion. Add broth and spices, and let simmer for 10 minutes or until the squash is soft. Remove from heat, and pour in the cream of your choice, adding more if you like a thinner consistency or less if you prefer a thicker one. Puree using an immersion blender or transfer to a regular blender and blend until smooth. Season with sea salt and pepper to taste.

If you can't find a butternut squash or are short on time, use frozen pre-cut butternut squash cubes or 1 can of pureed pumpkin instead. This soup makes a great side dish for meat, with added beans or other veggies.

TUSCAN WHITE BEAN STEW

MAKES ABOUT

8

SERVINGS

2	cans organic cannellini or white beans, rinsed and drained
6	small red or white potatoes, cubed
1/4	pound green beans, ends trimmed
3	roma tomatoes, diced
3	stalks celery, chopped
1	large or 2 small carrots, chopped
1/2	onion, chopped
3	cups organic chicken or vegetable stock
8	ounces tomato sauce
2	cloves garlic, chopped
1	tablespoon dried rosemary or 2 tablespoons fresh rosemary
1	teaspoon balsamic vinegar

Other great additions to this amazing stew would be chopped yams or sweet potatoes, shredded chicken or sausage, or a dollop of whole milk greek yogurt, sour cream, or pesto.

DIRECTIONS

Heat a bit of olive oil in a soup pot over medium heat. Add onion first, then after a few minutes, add carrots, celery and potatoes. After 4 additional minutes, add the white beans, tomatoes, tomato sauce, garlic, rosemary, green beans, and broth. Turn heat to high, and bring to a boil. Once boiling, immediately reduce heat to a simmer, and cover for 10-15 minutes until the potatoes are soft enough to poke with a fork. Season with sea salt and pepper to taste. Add a splash of balsamic vinegar right before serving.

SOUPS

POBLANO QUINOA CHICKEN CHILI

MAKES ABOUT

SERVINGS

- 1 cup shredded chicken or 4 links organic chicken sausage (pre-cooked)
- 1 can black, white, or kidney beans, rinsed and drained
- 1 poblano pepper, cubed
- 1 red bell pepper, cubed
- 2 zucchini, cubed
- 2 carrots, chopped
- 3 stalks celery, chopped
- 1 onion, chopped
- 2 cups organic chicken stock
- 1/2 cup dry quinoa
- 1 64 ounce can fire-roasted crushed tomatoes
- 1/2 teaspoon garam masala powder
- 1 teaspoon roasted chili powder
- \+ sea salt and pepper to taste

DIRECTIONS

In a stock pot, heat a generous splash of olive oil over medium heat. Add sliced sausage pieces; cook until brown on all sides. Remove the sausage and set aside.

Add chopped celery and onion into the pot, and let cook on medium heat for 3-4 minutes. Then add carrots and cook for another 3-4 minutes. Add peppers and cook for 5 more minutes.

Add chopped zucchini, roasted tomatoes, and chicken stock, plus 1 cup water. Add quinoa, cooked sausage or shredded chicken, chili powder, sea salt, pepper, and garam masala powder. Turn the heat up, cover, and let water come to a boil, then reduce to a low simmer for 15-20 minutes until the quinoa is cooked through. Soup is done when the quinoa softens, expands and naturally thickens to a stew-like texture.

With the quinoa added, this chili is very thick and hearty—almost like a stew. If you can't find poblano peppers, use a green bell pepper and jalapeño instead. Serve with avocado, chopped green onions, organic sour cream, or whole milk greek yogurt.

SPLIT PEA + CARROT SOUP

MAKES ABOUT

4

SERVINGS

1 1/2	cups dried split peas
1	carton of vegetable or organic chicken broth (approximately 4 cups)
3	stalks celery, chopped
2	carrots, chopped
1/2	onion, chopped
1	clove garlic, chopped
2	tablespoons fresh dill, chopped
1	teaspoon pepper
1/2	teaspoon sea salt

DIRECTIONS

In a soup pot, sauté onion with olive oil. Add garlic after 2-3 minutes. Add carrots and celery, and sauté until they begin to soften. Add soaked split peas and broth. Cover pot with a lid, and bring to a boil. When boiling, reduce heat to medium-low and simmer covered for 25 minutes, or until the peas are soft. Garnish with fresh chopped dill.

This is a blended soup, but can easily be kept chunky if you prefer (as pictured)—just make sure to cut the onion, celery, and carrots into similar sizes if you choose to do so. If possible, soak the split peas in water for 6-8 hours before cooking. If you don't have time, at least give them a good rinse before cooking.

COCONUT CORN CHOWDER

MAKES ABOUT
8
SERVINGS

6	ears organic corn, shucked and kernels sliced off the cob
1	pint baby tomatoes, whole
2	red peppers, chopped
1	sweet yellow onion, chopped
3	cloves garlic, chopped
1	8 ounce can coconut milk
2	cups organic vegetable or chicken broth
1/2	teaspoon cayenne
1/2	teaspoon Hungarian paprika or chili powder
+	sea salt and pepper to taste

DIRECTIONS

Set oven to a low or medium broil. Place tomatoes on a parchment-lined baking sheet. Drizzle with olive oil, add sea salt and pepper, then hand-toss to make sure the tomatoes are well-coated. Place in oven for approximately 10-15 minutes, or until tomatoes start to brown and blister.

Add chopped onion and garlic to a large soup pot with a dollop of olive or coconut oil, and sauté on medium heat for a few minutes until fragrant. Add the peppers first, then the corn, then the oven roasted tomatoes. After 5 minutes, add coconut milk, broth, and spices and stir. Let simmer for a few minutes before serving. For a smoother consistency, use an immersion blender to blend (fully or partially) before serving.

SOUPS

Serve hot or cold, garnished with fresh herbs like basil, cilantro, or parsley. Or make it a meal by adding shredded chicken, shrimp, grilled salmon or halibut pieces to the soup or serve on the side. If you are short on time, skip roasting the tomatoes, and add them in raw at the same time as the rest of the ingredients.

> FOOD HAS SO MANY COLORS... AND SO MANY FLAVORS. **I LOVE IT.** LET'S FACE IT: YOU DON'T HAVE TO DO MUCH TO FOOD WHEN IT ALREADY STARTS OUT LIKE ART.

WATERMELON-CUCUMBER GAZPACHO

- 1 three pound seedless watermelon or 5 cups, cubed
- 1 small cucumber, peeled, seeded, diced
- 1 red bell pepper, diced
- 1 yellow bell pepper, diced
- 1 jalapeño pepper, seeded, minced
- 3 pale green inner celery stalks, diced
- 1/2 small red onion, diced
- 1/2 cup fresh mint, finely chopped
- 3 tablespoons fresh lime juice
- 2 tablespoons red wine vinegar
- \+ sea salt and pepper to taste

MAKES ABOUT

10

SERVINGS

DIRECTIONS

Add all ingredients to a blender. Blend to your desired consistency and serve chilled. Optional to garnish with extra chopped mint.

I love this refreshing gazpacho soup, especially for summer parties. Serve in small glass jars or shot glasses for an easy and beautiful presentation!

HEARTY LENTIL STEW

MAKES ABOUT 8 SERVINGS

- 2 cups dried french lentils
- 6 cups organic chicken or vegetable broth
- 1 onion, chopped
- 2 carrots, chopped
- 6 stalks celery, chopped
- 8 white or cremini mushrooms, washed and sliced
- 2 tablespoons fresh thyme or 2 teaspoons dried
- 1 tablespoon sherry vinegar or white wine
- 1 teaspoon pepper
- 1/2 teaspoon sea salt

For a family dinner, set up a toppings bar so everyone can add their own twist.

DIRECTIONS

There is something so comforting about this classic lentil stew recipe. Maybe it's because it's the perfect vehicle for your own additions. This one is excellent paired with grilled chicken or sausage, avocado slices, grated parmesan cheese, millet or sprouted grain bread, a dollop of sour cream, whole milk greek yogurt, homemade pesto, or a **Mixed Green Salad**.

Ahead of time, add dry lentils to a large bowl and fill the bowl completely with water. Let soak for at least 6 hours and up to 24 hours before draining and rinsing.

When you're ready to cook, sauté onion, carrots, and celery with a tablespoon of olive oil in a large soup pot for about 5 minutes or until they start to brown. Remove these from the pot, add mushrooms with a bit more olive oil, and sauté on high heat until brown. Add a splash of white wine or sherry vinegar. Then, add the carrot, celery, and onion back to the soup pot with broth, soaked lentils, thyme, sea salt and pepper. Cover and bring to a boil, then reduce heat to medium-low for 15 minutes or until the lentils are soft.

MULLIGATAWNY SOUP

1	head cauliflower, stem removed and large florets chopped
1/2	head green cabbage, core removed and finely chopped
2	cans garbanzo beans, rinsed and drained
4	cloves garlic, chopped
4	carrots, chopped
1	large sweet potato, cubed
1	granny smith apple, cubed
1	onion, chopped
1	28 ounce can diced tomatoes
1	carton or 4 cups organic vegetable or chicken stock
2	teaspoons curry powder
1	teaspoon cumin
1	tablespoon fresh ginger, grated
1	teaspoon sea salt
1	teaspoon pepper
1/2	teaspoon cayenne pepper

MAKES ABOUT 8 SERVINGS

DIRECTIONS

Drizzle a bit of olive oil in a large soup pot over medium heat; sauté onion and garlic until fragrant. Add carrots, sweet potato, and cauliflower. After a few minutes, add apple, cabbage, tomatoes, stock, beans, and spices. Cover, turn up the heat, and bring to a boil. Once boiling, reduce heat to a simmer for 5-10 minutes or until the sweet potatoes can be easily poked with a fork.

A mix between a spicy and sweet curry and more mild vegetable soup, this Mulligatawny is a great way to eat lots of vegetables that will naturally fill you up. Optional to add quinoa, different types of beans, or shredded chicken. Great with avocado on top (obviously).

WHITE BEAN + CHICKEN CHILI VERDE

MAKES ABOUT

6

SERVINGS

- 4 thin organic chicken breasts (or 2 large breasts, cooked longer)
- 3 cans white northern beans, rinsed and drained
- 1 jalapeño, seeds removed and chopped
- 1 green pepper, chopped
- 1 onion, chopped
- 3 cloves garlic, chopped
- 1 24 ounce jar of green salsa
- 4 cups water, organic chicken broth, or vegetable broth
- 1 teaspoon pepper
- 1/2 teaspoon sea salt

To make this chili more spicy, use a medium or hot green salsa and keep the jalapeño seeds intact. To make in a slow cooker, add all ingredients together, and set on high for 4-6 hours, or low for 8-10 hours. Perfect garnished with cilantro and avocado.

DIRECTIONS

Preheat oven to 400°F. On a parchment-lined baking sheet or in a shallow glass baking dish, place chicken breasts and rub with a bit of olive oil. Sprinkle with sea salt and pepper and bake for 10-15 minutes until cooked through.

In a soup pot, heat a tablespoon of olive oil over medium heat and sauté onion and garlic for approximately 3-5 minutes. Add jalapeño and green pepper and sauté for another 3-4 minutes. Add beans, salsa, and water or broth; stir and cover. Turn heat up to high. Once boiling, reduce heat to simmer. Remove chicken from oven, shred into pieces, and add into soup. Garnish and serve.

SOUPS

RUSTIC VEGETABLE + BEAN CHILI

MAKES ABOUT

SERVINGS

1	can kidney beans (or any other type of bean)
1	can white beans (or any other type of bean)
6-8	baby Yukon potatoes, quartered
4	stalks celery, chopped
2	carrots, chopped
1	red bell pepper, chopped
1	green bell pepper, chopped
1	onion, chopped
1	carton or 4 cups organic chicken or vegetable stock
2	teaspoons garam masala
1	teaspoon chili powder
1	teaspoon pepper
1/2	teaspoon sea salt

DIRECTIONS

In a soup pot over medium heat, sauté onion in a tablespoon of olive oil for a few minutes. Then, add carrots and celery and let cook for another few minutes. Add peppers, potatoes, rinsed and drained beans, stock, and seasonings. Turn heat to high, and bring to a boil. Once boiling, reduce heat to a simmer and cover for 10-15 minutes until the potatoes are cooked through.

This vegetarian chili is great with added avocado, cooked brown or wild rice, or meat if you prefer.

TOMATO-BASIL SOUP

MAKES ABOUT

6

SERVINGS

- 1   28 ounce can of crushed tomatoes or 2 cups roasted and pureed tomatoes
- 4   ounces or ¼ cup basil leaves, chopped
- 2   large onions, chopped
- 1   clove garlic, chopped
- 1   cup organic chicken or vegetable broth
- 1/4   cup water
- 1   teaspoon pepper
- 1/2   teaspoon sea salt

DIRECTIONS

Add a tablespoon of olive oil to a soup pot over medium heat. Add chopped onions and stir occasionally until they are almost translucent. Add garlic. Then, stir in tomatoes, chicken broth, water, and pepper. Cover and let simmer for 5 minutes.

Remove from heat, add basil, and let cool for 10 minutes. Purée with a blender, or keep it chunky for a more rustic soup.

I love this simple and, I'd say, perfect tomato soup! For a heartier meal, add grilled chicken, or more roasted or fresh vegetables. Or, add a splash of coconut milk or whole milk for a creamier consistency.

MOROCCAN LAMB OR VEGGIE STEW

MAKES ABOUT 10 SERVINGS

- 1 pound organic ground lamb, turkey, beef, or pork
- 4 cans garbanzo beans, rinsed and drained
- 2 small sweet potatoes, cubed
- 1 carrot, grated or chopped
- 1 onion, chopped
- 10 dried dates or dried apricots, chopped
- 1/4 cup kalamata olives
- 2 tablespoons ginger root, grated
- 2 cloves garlic, pressed or chopped
- 1 28 ounce can crushed tomatoes
- 4 cups organic chicken or vegetable broth
- 1 tablespoon paprika (or smoked paprika)
- 2 teaspoons cumin
- 2 teaspoons cinnamon
- 2 teaspoons pepper
- 1/2 teaspoon sea salt

DIRECTIONS

In a soup pot, heat a dollop of coconut oil or a tablespoon of olive oil over medium heat. Add onion and garlic and sauté for 3-4 minutes. Add ground meat and sauté until almost cooked through. Then, add grated ginger and carrots. After 3 minutes, add sweet potatoes, olives, dates or apricots, tomatoes, broth, beans, and spices. Bring to a boil, then reduce to a simmer and cover for 30 minutes.

This hearty stew is great served on its own, or over cooked quinoa or rice. It can also be made with or without meat. If you want to make this in a slow cooker, start with the meat on the bottom, and add the rest of the ingredients on top. This soup tastes best the next day, so make it ahead of time if you can! Garnish with cilantro or greens.

CLASSIC CHICKEN AND VEGETABLE SOUP

- 2 cups organic **Shredded Chicken**
- 1/2 head green cabbage, chopped or shredded
- 3 carrots, chopped
- 3 stalks celery, chopped
- 1/2 onion, chopped
- 2-4 cups organic chicken broth
- 1 teaspoon dried sage
- 1 teaspoon dried parsley
- 1 teaspoon pepper
- 1/2 teaspoon sea salt

MAKES ABOUT

SERVINGS

DIRECTIONS

In a soup pot over medium heat, sauté onion in olive oil for 2-3 minutes. Add carrots, celery, cabbage, shredded chicken, and spices. Let cook for a few more minutes. Add the chicken broth, reduce the heat to a simmer, and let cook for 5-10 minutes.

*You won't even miss the noodles in this hearty and healing soup! You can easily make your own chicken (see **Easy Shredded Chicken** recipe), or to speed up the prep time, use a pre-cooked rotisserie chicken. Add brown rice or quinoa if you prefer a thicker soup.*

Whether you're cooking for yourself or people you love, these main meal dishes are perfect for quick weeknight dinners or dinner party dishes. That's the beauty of them. They are filling, delicious, and so satisfying, no matter who you're feeding.

the main MEAL

Garlic-Ginger Larb Lettuce Wraps **174**

Eggplant Bolognese Lasagna **178**

Butternut Squash, Salmon + Vegetable Curry **180**

Coconut-Almond Crusted Chicken **182**

Zucchini Pasta Noodles **184**

Pesto Chicken + Veggie Bake **186**

Mustard Roasted Fish + Fennel **188**

Baked Spaghetti Squash **190**

Organic Greek Meatballs **192**

Fajita Stir Fry **194**

Organic Turkey Meatloaf **196**

Black Bean and Spinach Enchilada Bake **198**

Grilled Flank Steak with Chimichurri Sauce + Blanched Green Beans **200**

Roasted Cherry Balsamic Chicken, Green Beans + Potatoes **202**

Molasses Ginger Salmon **204**

Mini Lamb, Turkey or Beef Sliders **206**

Jamaican Jerk Pineapple Chicken **208**

Pizza Quinoa Bites **210**

Parmesan Crusted Chicken Fingers **212**

Cauliflower Steaks **214**

Grilled Fish with Spring Pea + Mint Puree **216**

Spiced Black Beans + Fried Plantains **220**

Quinoa Stuffed Baked Tomatoes **222**

Cauliflower Crust Pizza **224**

Shrimp + Sausage Quinoa Paella **226**

Fried Ratatouille **228**

Maple-Hot Sauce Grilled Chicken with Grilled Peaches **230**

Grilled Fish with Mango Jalepeno Pineapple Salsa **232**

Easy Shredded Chicken **234**

GARLIC GINGER LARB LETTUCE WRAPS

MAKES ABOUT 6 SERVINGS

- 1 pound organic ground turkey, beef or chicken
- 2 cloves garlic, whole
- 1 2 inch ginger root, peeled
- 1 cucumber, peeled into ribbons
- 1 carrot, peeled into ribbons
- 1 head iceberg or butter lettuce, washed and separated into whole leaves
- 2 tablespoons crushed peanuts

DIRECTIONS

In a skillet, heat a dollop of coconut oil or tablespoon of olive oil over medium heat. Add ground meat of your choice and sauté until cooked through, grating the garlic and ginger with a cheese grater over the pan as you go. Sprinkle with sea salt. To serve, spoon ground meat onto lettuce leaves, top with cucumber, carrot ribbons and salad dressing or the *Peanut Sauce.* Garnish with crushed peanuts and extra dipping sauce.

*Larb is a classic Thai dish, and this is my favorite healthy upgrade of it, minus all the excessive salt and soy sauce. It's excellent paired with **Peanut Sauce**, hummus, salsa, guacamole, or avocado slices.*

> IF IT'S MARKETED TO YOU AS HEALTHY FOOD, CHANCES ARE THAT IT'S NOTHING CLOSE. READ THAT INGREDIENT LIST, PEOPLE. IT'S THE REAL DEAL.

EGGPLANT BOLOGNESE LASAGNA

LASAGNA

- 2 medium or 4 small Japanese eggplants
- 1 cup shredded mozzarella or parmesan cheese

BOLOGNESE SAUCE

- 1/2 pound organic ground turkey or chicken sausage (or 4 sausage links, sliced)
- 1 16 ounce can of tomato sauce or 6 roma tomatoes, roughly chopped
- 6 stalks celery, diced
- 2 carrots, diced or 1/2 cup shredded carrots
- 1 onion, finely chopped
- 1/2 cup fresh thyme or basil, chopped
- \+ sea salt and pepper to taste

MAKES ABOUT

SERVINGS

DIRECTIONS

Preheat oven to 400°F. Slice eggplant into thin rounds, approximately ¼ inch thick. Thinner is better so they cook faster.

In a large skillet, heat a little butter or olive oil over high heat. Add eggplant slices, and fry on each side until brown. Set aside.

Lower the heat slightly, add more oil or butter to the pan as well as the diced onion and sausage. Stir frequently to prevent burning, approximately 5 minutes. Add tomatoes, celery, carrots, and herbs and stir frequently for another 3-4 minutes. Reduce heat to a low simmer and cover until tomatoes can be crushed with a spoon. Set sauce aside to cool.

Next, grease or spray a small glass or ceramic baking dish. Add a layer of eggplant noodles to the bottom and sprinkle with cheese. Add a layer of the Bolognese sauce and fresh herbs. Keep repeating these layers until you run out of eggplant. Sprinkle more cheese on the top and bake for 10-15 minutes. Broil on high until the crust becomes brown and bubbly.

This Bolognese sauce is phenomenal, but if you are short on time, you can substitute a clean, jarred version instead. A mandoline slicer comes in handy for this recipe, but it's not necessary.

BUTTERNUT SQUASH, SALMON + VEGETABLE CURRY

MAKES ABOUT

4

SERVINGS

SALMON DISH

- 4 fillets wild salmon
- 1 cup butternut squash cubes
- 1 cup frozen peas
- 1 cup other veggies of your choice (carrots, cabbage, eggplant, mushrooms, green beans, snow peas, chopped in similar sizes)
- 1/2 onion, chopped
- 2 cloves garlic, chopped
- 1 tablespoon fresh ginger, grated

CURRY SAUCE

- 2 tablespoons red curry paste (or more or less, depending on your desired spice level)
- 8 ounces organic coconut milk
- + sea salt and pepper to taste

DIRECTIONS

Preheat oven to 400°F. In a large skillet, add onion, garlic, and ginger with a scoop of coconut oil or butter. Cook for 2-3 minutes, then add other veggies to the pan according to thickness and cooking time. Set aside when done.

In a separate large cast iron skillet, heat a bit of coconut oil on high heat. Let warm for 2-3 minutes until very hot. Sprinkle salmon with sea salt and pepper, and place flesh side down in the pan and cook for 2 minutes. Flip the fish, then transfer pan to the oven for 6 minutes.

Add curry paste and coconut milk together in small pot over low heat and whisk together. Add veggies to the salmon skillet and top with curry sauce.

Fresh cilantro, crushed cashews, peanuts, and limes all make great garnishes for serving. Using a cast iron skillet for the salmon is the best way to go for easy transferring from the stovetop into the oven. Excellent with brown or wild rice, or cooked quinoa to soak up the sauce!

Pan frying this chicken in a skillet will give you a crunchier texture, but if you're short on active cooking time, you can also lay the chicken pieces on a parchment-lined baking sheet and bake in the oven at 450°F, flipping halfway through, so each side browns nicely. Broil at the very end to darken the color. Try this recipe with white fish or shrimp too!

THE MAIN MEAL

COCONUT-ALMOND CRUSTED CHICKEN

4	organic, thin cut chicken breasts
1/2	cup small, unsweetened coconut flakes
1/2	cup almond meal or almond flour
1/4	teaspoon paprika
1/4	teaspoon lemon zest
1/4	teaspoon sea salt
1/4	teaspoon pepper

MAKES ABOUT

4

SERVINGS

DIRECTIONS

In a bowl, combine almond flour, coconut flakes, and spices. Rinse the chicken pieces, and pat dry with a paper towel. Drag the chicken through the coconut-almond mixture and place on a plate to rest. Heat a small bit of coconut oil in a skillet over medium-high heat. Cook each side equally; flipping halfway until both sides brown and the chicken is cooked through, approximately 4 minutes per side.

ZUCCHINI PASTA NOODLES

MAKES ABOUT 4 SERVINGS

2 large or 4 small organic zucchini

DIRECTIONS

This dish can be served raw or heated, with your favorite pasta or salad toppings. Sun-dried tomatoes, tomato sauce, pesto, **Romesco Sauce**, **Pea and Mint Purée**, sausage, grilled chicken, shrimp, or chopped basil are a few great topping options. Or, use a simple mixture of olive oil, garlic, oregano, and red pepper flakes.

Use a vegetable peeler or spiralizer to peel zucchini into noodles. Add noodles to a paper or dish towel and squeeze out excess moisture. To serve raw, combine zucchini with toppings and sauce. To enjoy warm, heat a bit of olive oil in a skillet on medium-high heat, and cook for a few minutes before adding toppings and sauce of your choice.

THE MAIN MEAL

I love using my vegetable spiralizer for this recipe, but if you don't have one, you can also use a vegetable peeler to get a similar effect.

PESTO CHICKEN + VEGGIE BAKE

MAKES ABOUT 6 SERVINGS

- **1** 8 ounce jar of pesto or 1 cup homemade pesto
- **6** thin cut organic chicken breasts
- **1** bunch asparagus or ½ pound green beans, ends trimmed
- **1/2** pint baby tomatoes, halved
- **+** sprinkle of parmesan cheese or mozzarella cheese

DIRECTIONS

Preheat oven to 375°F. Cover the bottom of a baking dish with a thin layer of pesto. Rinse chicken and pat dry with a paper towel. Arrange the breast pieces close together in the baking dish, without overlapping them. Cover each with a thin layer of pesto.

Add asparagus or green beans on top of the chicken, down the middle of the pan. Add the baby tomatoes around the border. Spread whatever leftover pesto you have across the top. Sprinkle cheese on top.

Cover with foil and bake for 30-35 minutes. Check to make sure the chicken is cooked though. Remove the foil and broil on high for 6 minutes, or until the cheese browns and bubbles on top.

*This is a great one-pan dish. If you don't like pesto, use a tomato sauce. If you can't do dairy, try using the **Cashew Pesto Kale** sauce instead.*

THE MAIN MEAL

MUSTARD ROASTED FISH + FENNEL

FISH

- 2 ½ inch thick pieces of fish
- 1 fennel bulb (or another quick-cooking veggie like green beans, thinly sliced carrots, or peppers)

MUSTARD MARINADE

- 4 tablespoons olive oil
- 2 tablespoons dijon mustard
- 2 tablespoons red wine vinegar or 1 lemon, juiced
- 1 teaspoon sea salt
- 2 teaspoons pepper

MAKES ABOUT

2

SERVINGS

If you are cooking for picky palates, add 1 tablespoon honey to the marinade for a sweeter honey mustard sauce. If you don't like fish, this recipe works well with chicken too; just add a little bit of cooking time.

DIRECTIONS

This recipe works great for salmon or any wild white fish like rockfish, halibut or mahi-mahi. Stay away from varieties that are too thin, like sole.

Whisk all ingredients together. Set aside.

Preheat oven to 400°F. Line a rimmed baking sheet or roasting pan with parchment paper. Slice the bottom of the fennel bulb into ½ inch rings or ½ inch pieces. (Note that the green stalks will be a much stronger flavor than the white bulb, and both will mellow as they cook.)

Place the fennel slices on the baking sheet. Drizzle with some of the mustard marinade, reserving most for the fish. Toss with your hands to coat the fennel, and place in the oven for 5 minutes. When ready, add fish to the same pan and top with the remaining mustard marinade. Return to the oven for approximately 10 minutes, depending on the thickness of your fish.

BAKED SPAGHETTI SQUASH

MAKES ABOUT

2

LARGE SERVINGS

1 large spaghetti squash

DIRECTIONS

Spaghetti squash has a large oval shape and light yellow-colored skin. When cooked and scooped out, the flesh forms spaghetti-like noodles. Typically, it's only available in the fall and early winter seasons, but its mild taste makes it a great vehicle for whatever toppings and sauce you'd like.

Preheat oven to 400°F. Cut top stem and bottom end off the squash. Stand the squash upright and slice in half. Scoop out seeds and membranes. Rub each half with olive oil, and place cut side down on a baking sheet. Bake for 25 minutes or until you can easily poke through the skin with a fork. When done, remove from oven and scoop out the flesh. Serve inside squash shells for a great presentation!

Try Spaghetti Squash drizzled with olive oil, sea salt and pepper, and/or your favorite sauce, like tomato sauce, **Roasted Red Pepper Harissa,** *pesto, or a drizzle of truffle oil with herbs.*

ORGANIC GREEK MEATBALLS

MAKES ABOUT 30 1/2 IN. MEATBALLS

- 1 pound organic ground chicken, turkey, beef or pork
- 1/2 cup almond meal or almond flour
- 1 egg
- 2 tablespoons fresh chopped fresh dill or 3 teaspoons dried dill or Italian seasoning
- 2 teaspoons dijon mustard
- 1 teaspoon dried oregano
- 1 clove garlic, chopped
- 1/2 teaspoon pepper
- 1/4 teaspoon sea salt

*These meatballs are amazing on their own, in **Spaghetti Squash**, on salads, in soups or as a great snack or appetizer. Check out the **Romesco Sauce, Roasted Red Pepper Harissa**, and **Pesto**, all of which go great with this recipe!*

DIRECTIONS

Feel free to swap out the herbs here, or use brown rice or garbanzo bean flour instead of almond flour if you'd like.

Combine all ingredients together in a bowl and mix well to combine. Roll into small ½ to 1 inch balls. Heat coconut oil or butter in a wide skillet and add a few meatballs to the pan at a time, turning so each side browns, approximately 5-7 minutes each.

THE MAIN MEAL

FAJITA STIR FRY

FAJITAS

1. pound organic ground turkey, beef, shrimp or fish
2. bell peppers, sliced
1. onion, sliced

MEXICAN SEASONING

2. teaspoons garam masala spice
2. teaspoons cumin
1/2. teaspoon cayenne pepper
+ sea salt and pepper to taste

MAKES ABOUT

2

SERVINGS

DIRECTIONS

Add coconut or olive oil to a large sauté pan over medium heat. Add your choice of meat. Cook turkey, shrimp and fish thoroughly, then remove from the pan. Add veggies next. As they soften, add spices. Stir to combine and serve warm.

This dish is great on top of a salad, in lettuce wraps, or in corn, sprouted grain, or brown rice tortillas. Serve with avocado, salsa, sour cream, or beans. If you can't find garam masala in the spice section, use garlic and onion powder with a sprinkle of cinnamon instead.

This is one of my favorite dinner recipes. If you don't want to use chia seeds, you can use an egg instead, although you will get a slightly different and less crunchy texture. If you are using ground turkey, I think the dark meat tastes best in this recipe! Also, feel free to add in other shredded veggies. Serve with extra tomato sauce, mustard, or a natural ketchup.

ORGANIC TURKEY MEATLOAF

- 1 1/2 pounds organic ground turkey or ground grass fed beef
- 1/2 cup almond flour, garbanzo bean flour or brown rice flour
- 1/2 cup tomato sauce
- 1/4 medium onion or ½ small onion, roughly chopped
- 2 tablespoons assorted chopped herbs: parsley, mint, thyme and basil are all good choices
- 1 clove garlic, chopped
- 1 tablespoon chia seeds
- 1 tablespoon red-wine vinegar
- 2 teaspoons dijon mustard
- 1/2 teaspoon sea salt
- 1/2 teaspoon pepper

MAKES ABOUT

6

SERVINGS

DIRECTIONS

Preheat oven to 400°F. Spray a pie pan or loaf pan with olive oil or coconut oil. Add all ingredients in a mixing bowl and stir well to combine. Let sit for 5 minutes so the chia seeds can expand. Pour the mixture into the pan and distribute it evenly with the back of a spoon. Bake for 40-45 minutes until the meat is cooked through. Drain off any excess liquid before serving.

BLACK BEAN + SPINACH ENCHILADA BAKE

- 2 packages organic corn tortillas
- 1 can black beans, rinsed and drained
- 1 jar salsa of your choice
- 1 ripe avocado, sliced
- 1 small container goat cheese or 1 cup shredded artisan cheese of your choice
- 1 small container pre-washed spinach or 1 bunch fresh spinach
- 1 64 ounce jar natural enchilada sauce

MAKES ABOUT

SERVINGS

DIRECTIONS

This vegetable based lasagna is one of my favorite one-pan meals and a great sneaky way to eat more spinach. Other great additions would be to add meat of your choice—chicken, steak, or pork would all work great here, or chopped kale, onions, ricotta cheese or cilantro.

Preheat oven to 375°F. Grease a large rectangular glass or oven-proof baking dish with a bit of olive oil. Cover the bottom of the dish with enchilada sauce. Add a layer of corn tortillas, tearing them to fit if necessary.

Layer with crumbled goat cheese, black beans, spinach, salsa and avocado. Add another layer of corn tortillas and pour enchilada sauce over the top. Continue building layers, ending with tortillas on top and sauce poured over them. Sprinkle with cheese. Cover and bake for 20-25 minutes.

Remove foil. Place back in oven for 5 minutes or until cheese browns and bubbles. Broil for the last minute or two for a nice crispy brown top layer.

Cleaner versions of enchilada sauce can be easily found at any natural food store, just be sure to read your ingredients.

GRILLED FLANK STEAK
with CHIMICHURRI SAUCE + BLANCHED GREEN BEANS

MAKES ABOUT 4 SERVINGS

This sauce is also great with beef, chicken, fish, shrimp, potatoes, or quinoa.

GRILLED FLANK STEAK

- 1 pound organic grass-fed flank steak
- 1/2 pound green beans, ends trimmed and cut in half

CHIMICHURRI SAUCE

- 1 bunch parsley, leaves only
- 1 bunch cilantro, leaves only
- 3 tablespoons capers
- 2 garlic cloves
- 1/2 cup olive oil
- 1 1/2 tablespoons white wine vinegar
- 1/2 teaspoon red pepper flakes
- 1/2 teaspoon ground black pepper
- 1 teaspoon sea salt
- 1 teaspoon pepper

DIRECTIONS

For a more traditional chimichurri sauce, chop all ingredients finely by hand and mix with olive oil. If you are short on time, add all ingredients to a blender, and pulse or blend to your desired consistency.

Ahead of time: in a plastic bag or glass baking dish, cover the steak with the chimichurri sauce (saving most of it for a topping after the meat is cooked), for up to 24 hours before cooking.

When ready to eat: heat a skillet, grill pan, or BBQ to medium-high heat. Add a bit of butter, olive oil or coconut oil to the pan, and wait for the heat source to warm up. While you wait, bring 2-3 cups of water to boil in a large pot (for green beans). Add steak to the hot pan, and cook for 3-4 minutes per side, depending on the thickness of the steak and your taste preference. When water boils in the green bean pot, add green beans and cover to cook for 2-3 minutes only. Then, drain and rinse the beans with cold water. When the steak is done, remove it from the heat, and let stand 2-3 minutes before slicing against the grain.

Drizzle your green beans with olive oil and sprinkle with sea salt and pepper to serve. Top steak with chimichurri sauce to serve.

ROASTED CHERRY BALSAMIC CHICKEN

with GREEN BEANS + POTATOES

MAKES ABOUT

6

SERVINGS

ROASTED CHICKEN, POTATOES + GREEN BEANS

- 6 organic chicken thighs
- 6 baby potatoes, cut into bite sized pieces
- 1/4 pound green beans, ends trimmed
- + chopped cilantro or mint for garnish (optional)
- + **Cherry Balsamic Sauce**

CHERRY BALSAMIC SAUCE

- 1/2 cup pitted cherries (frozen and defrosted are fine)
- 6 tablespoons balsamic vinegar
- 2 tablespoons olive oil
- 2 cloves garlic
- 1 teaspoon pure maple syrup
- 1 teaspoon dijon mustard
- + sea salt and pepper to taste

DIRECTIONS

Combine all sauce ingredients in a blender. Blend until mostly smooth. Marinate the chicken thighs with the sauce in a plastic bag or glass dish (reserving a bit of sauce for drizzling on the cooked chicken) for at least 5 minutes and up to 24 hours before cooking. The longer it marinates, the more flavorful the meat will be.

Preheat oven to 425°F. Drizzle the bottom of a glass baking dish with olive oil. Add marinated chicken. Add the potatoes and green beans around the chicken. Drizzle a bit of olive oil, and add a pinch of sea salt and pepper to the veggies. Toss to coat with your hands. Bake for approximately 25-30 minutes, depending on the thickness of the chicken. When done, broil for 1-2 minutes until the chicken browns nicely on top. Garnish with chopped cilantro or mint to serve.

THE MAIN MEAL

This is a great sauce to make a double batch of and use on other roasted veggies, quinoa, millet, brown rice, meat fish, or even on ice cream!

Fun fact: blackstrap molasses has great health enzymes and minerals that you can't get anywhere else. Make good use of its smoky flavor with this amazing marinade for grilled or roasted fish. Just be sure to remove the fish from the heat 1-2 minutes before it looks done, as it will continue cooking when you take it out.

MOLASSES GINGER SALMON

- 1 12 ounce wild salmon filet
- 4 tablespoons fresh ginger, grated
- 2 cloves garlic, chopped
- 2 tablespoons unrefined sesame oil
- 2 tablespoons unrefined blackstrap molasses
- 1 teaspoon chili powder
- + sea salt and pepper to taste

MAKES ABOUT 2 SERVINGS

DIRECTIONS

If you don't like fish, try this same sauce combination over rice, quinoa or vegetables.

Preheat oven to 350°F, or preheat a grill to medium heat. In a bowl, mix together sesame oil, chili powder, sea salt, pepper and garlic. Add molasses and grated ginger, and whisk ingredients together, melting the molasses if necessary.

Rinse the salmon, pat dry with a paper towel and place on a parchment lined baking sheet. Pour the molasses-ginger marinade over the fish. Cook on the grill or in the oven at a medium temperature for about 8-10 minutes, or until the thicker part of the fish is almost opaque.

Remove from the oven and let sit covered for 2-3 minutes before serving.

Serve these burgers on their own, or with toasted sprouted grain or millet bread. Perfect with **the Cucumber Yogurt Dressing** *or other homemade dressing of your choice. Top with sliced avocado, onion, sun-dried tomatoes, mustard, sauerkraut, clean ketchup, pickles, artisan cheese slices, or organic bacon to serve.*

MINI LAMB, TURKEY OR BEEF SLIDERS

MAKES ABOUT

12

MINI BURGERS

- 1 pound organic ground lamb, turkey or beef
- 1/2 small sweet onion, chopped
- 1 clove garlic, chopped
- 1 16 ounce can tomato sauce
- 2 tablespoons chopped parsley or 1 teaspoon dried Italian herbs
- + sea salt and pepper to taste

DIRECTIONS

Combine all ingredients in a bowl, and mix to combine with your hands. Form meat into small patties and fry stovetop on medium-high heat until cooked through to your liking. You can also cook these on the grill if your grates are close enough together. If your meat is not sticking together, try adding an egg or a few teaspoons of chia seeds to the mix.

JAMAICAN PINEAPPLE JERK CHICKEN

MAKES ABOUT

SERVINGS

CHICKEN

- 4 organic chicken breasts
- 1 can crushed pineapple or ½ fresh pineapple, sliced

SPICE RUB

- 1 teaspoon allspice
- 1 teaspoon cumin
- 1 teaspoon cinnamon
- 1/2 teaspoon thyme
- 1/2 teaspoon cayenne pepper
- 1/2 teaspoon sea salt
- 1/2 teaspoon pepper

DIRECTIONS

Mix all spice rub ingredients together in a small bowl. Add in 3 tablespoons of olive oil, and mix well to combine. Rinse chicken breasts, and lightly pat dry with a paper towel. Rub each breast with the spice sauce, or add with pineapple to a plastic bag to let marinate for at least 30 minutes and up to 24 hours before serving. Grill or cook on the stovetop over medium heat.

Feel free to add in other veggies to grill or roast. Asparagus, green beans, peppers, green onions, carrots and sweet potatoes would all work great in this recipe! The jerk seasoning also makes a great rub for pork, steak, fish and seafood. Marinade can be prepared up to 24 hours in advance.

PIZZA QUINOA BITES

MAKES ABOUT

12 MUFFINS

OR

24 MINI MUFFINS

- 1 cup dry quinoa
- 1/2 cup cheese, grated plus more to sprinkle on the top
- 3 ounces tomato sauce
- 1 egg
- 2 teaspoons Italian seasoning or 1 tablespoon fresh chopped basil, oregano or parsley
- 1 teaspoon garlic powder or 1 garlic clove, chopped
- 1 teaspoon paprika
- + sprinkle of red pepper flakes (optional)
- + sea salt and pepper to taste

This is a great basic recipe to build off of. Add whatever other pizza "toppings" you like: olives, peppers, cooked mushrooms, sausage, pesto, pineapple, etc.

DIRECTIONS

If you are dairy free, add 1 teaspoon chia seeds to 6 teaspoons water in a small bowl and let soak for 3-4 minutes before adding to the mix instead of cheese. Then add 3 teaspoons nutritional yeast as well for extra flavor! Serve with extra tomato or pesto sauce for dipping.

Preheat oven to 350°F. Cook quinoa by adding it to a pot with 2 cups of water. Sprinkle with sea salt, cover, and bring to a boil. Once boiling, turn off heat and let sit for 10 minutes until all the water is absorbed. Spray or line a mini or regular muffin tin.

Combine all ingredients in a bowl, adding warm cooked quinoa last. Stir well, and add the batter into the muffin tins. Sprinkle each muffin with a bit of extra cheese. Bake for 25 minutes for regular muffins or 15 minutes for mini muffins, or until cheese is melted.

THE MAIN MEAL

PARMESAN CRUSTED CHICKEN

- **4** organic, thin cut chicken breasts or 2 large chicken breasts, sliced
- **4** tablespoons almond flour, almond meal or brown rice flour
- **4** tablespoons grated parmesan cheese
- **2** teaspoons Italian herb seasoning
- **2** teaspoons pepper
- **1/2** teaspoon sea salt

MAKES ABOUT

SERVINGS

*This recipe is perfect on its own or paired with the **Romaine or Kale Caesar Salad.***

DIRECTIONS

Pan frying this chicken will give you a crunchier texture. If you're short on active cooking time, you can also lay the chicken breasts on a parchment-lined baking sheet and bake in the oven at 450°F, flipping halfway through, so each side browns nicely. Broil at the very end to darken the color. You can also try this recipe with shrimp or any wild white fish of your choice, or use nutritional yeast instead of cheese to keep it dairy free.

In a bowl, mix almond flour, cheese, and spices. Rinse chicken pieces and gently pat dry with a paper towel. Dip each piece of meat into the almond-cheese mixture. Press the mixture on all sides of the chicken and place on a plate to rest. Press any leftover mixture on top. Heat a scoop of coconut oil or a tablespoon of olive oil in a skillet on medium-high heat and fry chicken on each side until crispy and brown on the outside.

Think vegetables can't be filling as a main meal? Then you haven't tried these yet. These "steaks" are great on their own, or with any toppings of your choice, including tomato sauce and meat, **Roasted Red Pepper Harissa Sauce**, pesto, **Chimichurri Sauce**, chopped garlic with lemon juice, olive oil and red pepper flakes, olive tapenade or an eggplant tapenade. Pictured here over tomato sauce.

CAULIFLOWER STEAKS

MAKES ABOUT

SERVINGS

1 large head cauliflower

DIRECTIONS

Preheat oven to 425°F. Line a baking sheet with parchment paper. Trim leaves and bottom stem off of cauliflower and discard. Holding the cauliflower upright on a cutting board, make 1 inch slices (similar to bread slices). Carefully add each slice to the baking sheet.

Drizzle cauliflower slices with olive oil, sea salt and pepper, and gently rub each side. Be careful, they can crumble! Roast for 30 minutes or until brown. Add over or under your favorite warm sauce and toppings.

GRILLED FISH with SPRING PEA + MINT PUREE

MAKES ABOUT

SERVINGS FISH
AND

SERVINGS PUREE

FISH

1   large piece of wild white fish

SPRING PEA + MINT PUREE

1   16 ounce package of frozen peas
1/2   cup shredded parmesan cheese
1/2   onion, roughly chopped
10   large leaves of fresh mint
4   tablespoons organic melted butter or olive oil
1   clove garlic
1   teaspoon pepper
1/4   teaspoon sea salt

DIRECTIONS

- For the sauce -

Add frozen peas, chopped onion, and garlic clove to a saucepan. Add enough water to cover them and bring to a boil. Cook according to the pea package, approximately 3-4 minutes. Drain when ready. Add peas, onion and garlic to a blender with melted butter or olive oil, mint, sea salt and pepper. Add a tiny bit of water if needed to blend. Adjust seasonings as necessary.

- For the fish -

Heat a scoop of coconut oil or a tablespoon of olive oil in a skillet over medium-high heat, or preheat the grill. Fry fish on both sides or cook until done to your liking. Serve with puree over the top.

This sauce freezes well too, so feel free to make extra and freeze to use on other roasted veggies, meat, fish, quinoa, brown rice, etc. If you are dairy free, use 2 teaspoons nutritional yeast + 2 tablespoons almond, hemp or rice milk instead of the cheese.

> THE KEY TO A HEALTHIER LIFESTYLE? LISTENING TO YOUR OWN BODY. TAKING IT OUT OF AUTOPILOT AND ACTUALLY LISTENING TO WHAT IT'S SAYING, INSTEAD OF TRYING TO BOSS IT AROUND LIKE YOU KNOW BEST.

cilantro

plantains

feta

radishes

black beans

SPICED BLACK BEANS + FRIED PLANTAINS

- 2 plantains, sliced on a diagonal cut (approximately ½ inch per slice)
- 1 can black beans, rinsed and drained
- 2 teaspoons cumin
- 1 lime, juiced
- + sea salt and pepper to taste

MAKES ABOUT 2 SERVINGS

DIRECTIONS

Other optional toppings could include sliced radishes, crumbled **Meatloaf**, avocado, crumbled feta, chopped cilantro, feta cheese, hot sauce, **Romesco Sauce** or **Cilantro Avocado Sauce.**

Heat a skillet to medium-high heat, add a scoop of coconut oil or a tablespoon of olive oil to warm. Fry plantains on both sides, then top with beans. Sprinkle with sea salt, pepper, and cumin. Squeeze lime juice over the top right before serving. Garnish with cilantro to serve.

Plantains are usually found right by the bananas at the store—they look very similar but are browner and smaller in size. If you can't find them at your store, use a sweet potato instead, just give it a little bit more time to cook.

QUINOA STUFFED BAKED TOMATOES

MAKES ABOUT

SERVINGS

- 8 large tomatoes
- 1 cup dry quinoa or brown rice
- 2 cups fresh spinach (or more)
- 1/2 pound cooked crumbled organic sausage (optional)
- 1/2 cup feta, goat cheese or gorgonzola crumbled cheese
- 1/4 cup chopped basil or 1 teaspoon dried oregano/Italian seasoning
- 2 cloves garlic, finely chopped
- 1 teaspoon pepper
- 1/2 teaspoon sea salt

This is a perfect make-ahead dish for a crowd, and is easily adaptable to your own additions. If you don't like tomatoes, use peppers instead, just factor in a longer cooking time. If you do use tomatoes, try to pick slightly firmer ones at the store.

DIRECTIONS

Preheat oven to 425°F. Cook quinoa by combining ½ cup dry quinoa with 1 cup water and 2 dashes of sea salt and cover with a lid. As soon as water boils, reduce heat to the lowest possible simmer or turn heat completely off and keep covered. Let sit for 10 minutes until done.

Slice the top off of each tomato, and gently scoop the seeds out. Place in a glass or ceramic baking dish. If the tomatoes do not sit flat, slice a bit off the bottom.

In a skillet, sauté crumbled sausage first (if using), then add garlic and spinach until the spinach wilts. Add the warm ingredients to a large bowl, then add herbs, quinoa, cheese of your choice, sea salt and pepper, and mix to combine.

Fill each tomato with the quinoa stuffing, drizzle with a bit of olive oil, and top with a tiny bit of crumbled cheese. Bake for 20-25 minutes until done. Broil for the last 2-3 minutes to get a nice crispy brown layer on top. Serve hot or at room temperature.

THE MAIN MEAL

FOR THE CRUST

- 2 eggs
- 3/4 cup
- 2 TB
- 1 Med

# CAULIFLOWER PIZZA

FOR THE CRUST

- 1 large head cauliflower, florets only (approximately 3 cups)
- 3/4 cup grated parmesan cheese
- 2 tablespoons almond flour, brown rice flour or gluten free flour blend
- 2 eggs
- 1 teaspoon pepper
- 1/2 teaspoon sea salt

TO TOP

- 1 16 oz jar clean tomato sauce or pesto
- + other toppings of your choice: roasted red peppers or sun-dried tomatoes, pre-cooked organic sausage, organic mozarella, parmesan, feta or goat cheese.

MAKES ABOUT

4

SERVINGS

DIRECTIONS

Preheat oven to 450°F. Line a baking sheet with parchment paper. Add cauliflower florets to a powerful blender or food processor, and blend until smooth. Don't overprocess it, but blend enough so that you no longer have any big pieces visible.

Place the pulsed cauliflower in the middle of a clean dish towel. Wrap it up, and squeeze as much moisture out of it as you can. There will be a lot! Then, open the towel and place the cauliflower in a mixing bowl. Add the cheese, flour, egg and spices, and mix together. Combine the mixture into a ball.

With your hands, flatten dough into an even crust on the baking sheet. Bake for 20-25 minutes until it starts to brown. Remove from heat, add your sauce and toppings, and place back in the oven until done, depending on what toppings you choose. Broil at the end to brown the cheese for a great presentation.

If there ever was a healthier way to do pizza, this is it! You will need a clean dish towel to make this crust, as well as a powerful blender or food processor. If you don't have one, no problem— just boil the cauliflower florets before you blend them.

This is a great family style dish and one pan meal. Traditionally made with white rice, I've upgraded it with quinoa to cut down on the cooking time and give it a little bit more protein, but you can also try this recipe with black rice, wild rice or brown rice. Scallops, shrimp, mussels, clams, shredded pork or chicken would also work great in this recipe, depending on your tastes.

SHRIMP + SAUSAGE QUINOA PAELLA

4	links organic chicken or andouille sausage, sliced into coins
1/2	pound wild shrimp, pre-cooked
1 1/2	cups quinoa, brown, wild, or black rice plus 3 cups water
1	16 ounce can tomato sauce
1	cup frozen peas
1	bell pepper, sliced
10	cremini or white mushrooms, sliced
1	onion, chopped
2	cloves garlic, finely chopped
2	teaspoons smoked paprika
1	pinch saffron
1	lemon, sliced into wedges for serving
+	sea salt and pepper to taste
+	sprinkle of chili powder

MAKES ABOUT

SERVINGS

DIRECTIONS

Preheat oven to 400°F. In a large skillet, sauté onion and garlic until fragrant. Add mushrooms first, then peppers, and sauté until brown. In the meantime, cook quinoa: Add 3 cups water and 1 ½ cups quinoa with a few dashes of sea salt to a large soup pot, and bring to a boil. Once boiling, reduce heat to a low simmer and keep covered for 10 minutes. Fluff when done.

Remove veggies from pan and set aside. Add more oil to the pan and cook sausage and shrimp (you may have to do this one portion at a time depending on space). Add peas in the last 3 minutes of cooking. Set aside. Add quinoa, sea salt, pepper smoked paprika, saffron, tomato sauce, onions, and garlic to a large bowl. Stir well to combine, then add to an oven-proof skillet. Layer veggies, sausage, and shrimp on top to serve. Garnish with lemon wedges.

You can eat this recipe as a soup by adding 1 cup of tomato sauce and 1 cup of broth. Or, try any of the following: poached or fried eggs; with burrata, ricotta or mozarella cheese on gluten free toast; over brown rice pasta; over an arugula salad; or over grilled halibut. You can also try adding in some garbanzo beans for a slightly heavier meal.

FRIED RATATOUILLE

1	small eggplant, cubed
1	zucchini, cubed
1	summer squash, cubed
1	small red onion, cubed
1	red pepper, cubed
1 1/2	pint baby tomatoes
3	cloves garlic, roughly chopped
1/4	cup chopped basil, plus more to garnish
1/2	teaspoon red pepper flakes
+	splash of balsamic vinegar
+	sea salt and pepper to taste

MAKES ABOUT

SERVINGS

DIRECTIONS

Heat zucchini, squash, and pepper cubes over medium heat in a skillet with olive or coconut oil. Cook for approximately 5 minutes. In the meantime, heat eggplant cubes in a separate skillet (hint: this is the KEY to great, non-mushy eggplant), adding extra oil when needed. Cook for 5 minutes as well on medium-high heat. Add eggplant to the other veggies, and add garlic and tomatoes. Add basil; cover and cook for another 2-3 minutes until tomatoes soften. Season with red pepper flakes, sea salt, pepper, and balsamic vinegar. Serve as desired, with extra basil sprinkled over the top.

- To make Ratatouille Polenta Bites -

Slice a polenta roll into ½ inch circle slices. Fry on both sides in a hot skillet, until they begin to crisp and brown, approximately 10 minutes. Top with ricotta, mozarella or burrata cheese, the ratatouille mixture and drizzle with balsamic vinegar to serve. Garnish with chopped basil.

MAPLE HOT SAUCE GRILLED CHICKEN
with GRILLED PEACHES

MAKES ABOUT 4 CHICKEN BREASTS

CHICKEN

- 4 organic chicken breasts
- 2 peaches, semi-firm, cut in half or slices

MAPLE-HOT SAUCE

- 4 tablespoons maple syrup
- 4 tablespoons olive oil
- 1 tablespoon hot sauce (or more if you like it spicy)
- 1/2 teaspoon sea salt and pepper

This marinade works great for steak, shrimp and fish too! If peaches are not in season, use whatever fruit is, like apples, pears, plums, or berries, or veggies of your choice instead.

DIRECTIONS

Mix marinade ingredients together first, then place chicken and peaches in a shallow glass baking dish or plastic bag, and pour the marinade over the top for up to 24 hours before grilling. Pan fry on the stove or bake at 375°F, approximately 10-15 minutes or until chicken is cooked through.

THE MAIN MEAL

GRILLED FISH with MANGO JALAPEÑO PINEAPPLE SALSA

FISH

- **2** pieces wild white fish

MANGO JALAPEÑO SALSA

- **5** ripe mangos, peeled and cut into bite sized cubes (approximately 4 cups)
- **1** fresh pineapple, cut into bite sized cubes (approximately 3 cups)
- **1/2** red onion, very thinly sliced and chopped
- **2-3** jalapeños, seeded and chopped
- **1/2** cup chopped cilantro

MAKES ABOUT

4

SERVINGS FISH *AND*

8

SERVINGS SALSA

DIRECTIONS

- Mango Jalapeño Salsa -

Combine all ingredients in a bowl with a bit of sea salt and pepper. Cover and chill for a least 1 hour if you can before serving.

- Fish -

Grill fish in a skillet on medium-high heat with a scoop of coconut oil, or bake in the oven at 350°F for 7-10 minutes, depending on the thickness of the fish.

Serve this salsa over grilled fish or chicken, or straight up with organic corn chips, or for homemade ceviche. Keeps fresh for up to 3 days in the fridge.

EASY SHREDDED CHICKEN

MAKES ABOUT 4 SERVINGS

4 organic chicken breasts

DIRECTIONS

Bring a few cups of broth or water to a boil in a medium-sized pot with lid. Once boiling, add chicken breasts, reduce heat to medium and cover and let cook for 10-15 minutes or until the chicken can easily be pulled apart with a fork. Drain water and shred the rest of the chicken. Toss with olive oil, Italian herbs, sea salt, and pepper before serving.

This is a great way to prep chicken to use in a multitude of ways during the week. Add a homemade sauce or dressing once cooked, or keep it simple by drizzling with olive oil, herbs, sea salt, and pepper.

THE MAIN MEAL

vegetables + SIDE DISHES

Roasted Nutmeg Delicata Squash **238**

Olive Oil Mashed Potatoes with Garlic + Herbs **240**

Roasted Carrots or Parsnips with Honey, Cilantro + Lime **242**

Healthy Baked Beans **246**

Smashed Potatoes with Romesco Sauce **248**

Curry-Spiced Sweet Potato Fries **250**

Perfect Brussels Sprouts **252**

Roasted Spiced Cauliflower **254**

Spinach, Pea + Parmesan Bowls **256**

Shaved Asparagus Salad **258**

Twice-Baked Cinnamon Sweet Potatoes **260**

ROASTED NUTMEG DELICATA SQUASH

MAKES ABOUT

4

SERVINGS

3 medium delicata squash
1 tablespoon coconut oil, melted
1 teaspoon nutmeg
1/2 teaspoon sea salt

DIRECTIONS

Line a baking sheet with parchment paper. Preheat oven to 400°F. Wash squash, cut ends off, and slice lengthwise down the middle. Scoop out inner seeds, and discard (or save to roast separately).

Place squash cut-side down on a cutting board and slice into half-moon shapes. Spread on the baking sheet, drizzle with the melted coconut oil and sprinkle with nutmeg and sea salt. Roast for 20-25 minutes, tossing the pieces around mid-way until squash is slightly browned on all sides.

This recipe works great with other types of squash, but the delicata variety is the easiest to cut and has edible skin, which cuts down on the prep time. Optional to add chili powder, curry powder, or garam masala to kick up the spice factor! Also optional to garnish with pieces of fried organic bacon, sage, or a bit of maple syrup before serving. Serve hot or cold. Also great for breakfast.

VEGETABLES + SIDE DISHES

VEGETABLES + SIDE DISHES

OLIVE OIL MASHED POTATOES
with GARLIC + HERBS

MAKES ABOUT

6

SERVINGS

- **4** russet or 6 yukon gold potatoes, whole
- **1/2** cup olive oil
- **2** cloves garlic, whole
- **1/2** cup fresh herbs of your choice: parsley, tarragon, basil, dill, or rosemary

DIRECTIONS

In a large soup pot, bring enough water to a boil to cover the potatoes. Once boiling, add potatoes and cook for 15-20 minutes or until the potatoes are easily poked with a fork. Add garlic cloves to the pot in the last 5 minutes. Drain water, but reserve ½ cup of the cooking water in the pot. Mash potatoes with a hand masher, or blend with an immersion or regular blender to whatever consistency you like. Add olive oil, extra cooking water, herbs, and a generous amount of sea salt and pepper as you blend. Add more olive oil if necessary to taste.

Mashed potatoes, made healthy? You'll believe it when you taste these. Olive oil easily replaces the heavier cream, butter and flour in this decadent seeming and delicious rendition of a classic comfort dish. Great for the holidays too!

VEGETABLES + SIDE DISHES

ROASTED CARROTS + PARSNIPS
with HONEY, CILANTRO + LIME

MAKES ABOUT 5 SERVINGS

- 1 bunch carrots or parsnips, sliced in half lengthwise (approximately 12 carrots)
- 1 lime, juiced
- 3 tablespoons extra-virgin olive oil or melted butter
- 1 tablespoon cilantro leaves, chopped
- 3 teaspoons honey

DIRECTIONS

Preheat oven to 400°F and line a baking sheet with parchment paper. Whisk lime juice, honey, cilantro, and olive oil together in a small bowl, melting the honey first if necessary. Arrange carrots or parsnips evenly on baking sheet and drizzle with the honey-lime mixture. Roast for 25-30 minutes or until caramelized. Sprinkle with extra chopped cilantro to serve.

Try using multi-colored carrots to make this dish even more beautiful. This recipe also works great for almost any vegetable.

> MAKE YOUR VEGETABLES TASTE GOOD. ROAST THEM. GIVE THEM TEXTURE. PUT SOME BUTTER ON THEM. OR PARMESAN CHEESE OR TRUFFLE OIL. HERBS. BACON EVEN. SEA SALT AND PEPPER. MAKE THEM SEXY. NOT THE BORING SIDE DISH ON THE TABLE. YOU'LL PROBABLY WANT TO EAT MORE OF THEM, WHICH BUILDS A BETTER, MORE POSITIVE RELATIONSHIP WITH EATING HEALTHY FOOD, FOR PEOPLE OF ALL AGES. DO IT, YOU WON'T BE SORRY.

VEGETABLES + SIDE DISHES

HEALTHY BAKED BEANS

2	cans white, navy or cannellini beans, rinsed and drained
2	small yellow onions, chopped
4	cloves garlic, chopped
4	tablespoons tomato paste
2	tablespoons dijon mustard
2	tablespoons maple syrup
2	tablespoons molasses
1	cup water
+	sea salt and pepper to taste

MAKES ABOUT

6

SERVINGS

DIRECTIONS

In a skillet over low heat, sauté onion and garlic with olive oil until fragrant. Add tomato paste, mustard, maple syrup, molasses, and water. Stir. Add beans, reduce heat, and cover for 5-10 minutes before serving.

This is a great side dish anytime of year! Feel free to add organic nitrate-free bacon if you want some extra smoky flavor.

SMASHED POTATOES

VEGETABLES + SIDE DISHES

6 small yukon gold potatoes or 8 baby potatoes, whole

MAKES ABOUT

4

SERVINGS

DIRECTIONS

Add enough water to a pot to cover potatoes and bring to a boil. Once boiling, add potatoes, reduce heat, and cover until potatoes are easily poked with a fork, approximately 10 minutes. Drain and let cool. Smash each potato flat with a masher or fork, keeping each intact as much as possible. Heat a generous amount of olive oil in a skillet and fry the potatoes on both sides until crispy and brown. Serve warm or cold.

These are a perfect side dish for any dinner, brunch, or weekend breakfast. Amazing paired with the **Romesco Sauce** *(pictured) or* **Chimichurri Sauce**

CURRY-SPICED SWEET POTATO FRIES

- **1** large sweet potato
- **1-2** teaspoons curry powder
- **+** sea salt to taste

MAKES ABOUT

2

SERVINGS

DIRECTIONS

Preheat oven to 400°F. Line a baking sheet with parchment paper. Slice sweet potatoes into long sticks like French fries. Add to a large bowl and drizzle with olive oil, curry powder, and sea salt. Toss to coat well and spread out on a baking sheet. Bake for 25 minutes or until cooked through. Broil at the end if desired.

*If you don't like curry powder, try cinnamon and a bit of cayenne pepper instead. These fries are amazing dipped in natural ketchup, or in **Romesco Sauce** or **Roasted Red Pepper Harissa Sauce.***

VEGETABLES + SIDE DISHES

PERFECT BRUSSEL SPROUTS

2 cups brussels sprouts, sliced in half

MAKES ABOUT

4

SERVINGS

DIRECTIONS

Make crunchy and flavorful brussel sprouts at home with this easy recipe! Customize however you choose: plain with sea salt and pepper, with a drizzle of truffle oil and pepper, sprinkle with herbs and parmesan cheese, with fried bacon and maple syrup, or with sea salt and vinegar right before serving.

Preheat oven to 400°F. Heat a splash of olive oil in an ovenproof skillet over medium-high heat. Toss brussel sprout halves with a bit of olive oil, and arrange all of them face down on the hot skillet. Let cook for 3-4 minutes or until brown on the bottom. Flip sprouts and place into the oven for another 5 minutes, or until crispy. Garnish however you choose!

You will need an ovenproof skillet for this recipe, or you can transfer the sprouts to a parchment-lined baking sheet before placing in the oven.

ROASTED SPICED CAULIFLOWER

MAKES ABOUT 3 SERVINGS

- 1 large or 2 small heads of cauliflower, florets only (or 6 cups pre-cut cauliflower florets)
- 10 dried dates or prunes, sliced in half
- 5 cloves garlic, whole
- 1 teaspoon garam masala
- 1 teaspoon nutmeg
- + sea salt and pepper to taste
- + chopped fresh basil to garnish

This is a great little twist on a basic roasted cauliflower recipe. Also try this same method with olive oil and fresh chopped herbs or truffle oil and garlic.

DIRECTIONS

Preheat oven to 425°F. Line a baking sheet with parchment paper and add cauliflower florets, dates or prunes, and garlic in an even layer. Drizzle with olive oil and mix well with your hands to coat equally with oil. Sprinkle with garam masala, nutmeg, sea salt and pepper and roast until the cauliflower begins to brown, approximately 20 minutes.

VEGETABLES + SIDE DISHES

SPINACH, PEA + PARMESAN BOWLS

MAKES ABOUT **1** SERVING

- 1/4 cup quinoa
- 1/2 cup water
- 2 handfuls spinach, or more
- 1/4 cup frozen peas
- 1/4 cup parmesan cheese, grated
- + sea salt and pepper to taste

Unsure about quinoa? Try this recipe. It's my best take on a healthier mac n' cheese. With veggies, of course.

DIRECTIONS

Add quinoa, peas, a generous dash of sea salt, and water to a saucepan and bring to a boil. Once boiling, turn off heat and let sit for 10 minutes or until all the water is absorbed. Add spinach and parmesan cheese to the pot, and stir until the spinach wilts and cheese melts. Add more sea salt and pepper to taste before serving.

VEGETABLES + SIDE DISHES

SHAVED ASPARAGUS SALAD

MAKES ABOUT 2 SERVINGS

- 1 bunch thick asparagus
- 1 large lemon or 2 small lemons, juiced
- 1 small handful of sweet green herbs like basil, mint, or parsley
- + drizzle of olive oil
- + sea salt and pepper to taste

DIRECTIONS

Wash asparagus. Over a bowl or cutting board, use a potato peeler or julienne slicer to shave asparagus into pieces. Set aside pieces that get too small to shave and cut them instead with a small knife. Add all asparagus pieces to a bowl and drizzle with lemon juice, herbs, olive oil, sea salt, and pepper. Toss gently to combine.

This is a great spring or summer dish, and a more unique way to eat asparagus, especially when you buy a thick bunch. Great additions are slivered almonds, pine nuts, baby tomatoes, sundried tomatoes, artichoke hearts, meat, fish, shrimp, other veggies, or fresh shaved parmesan.

VEGETABLES + SIDE DISHES

VEGETABLES + SIDE DISHES

TWICE-BAKED CINNAMON SWEET POTATOES

MAKES ABOUT

4

SERVINGS

- **2** sweet potatoes or yams
- **2** tablespoons coconut oil or butter, melted
- **2** teaspoons cinnamon
- **+** sea salt to taste

DIRECTIONS

Preheat oven to 425°F. Slice a sweet potato in half lengthwise and rub with butter or melted coconut oil. Place face down on a baking sheet and bake for 20 minutes, or until easily poked with a fork. Remove from oven, flip potatoes flesh-side up, and mash the insides with more melted coconut oil, cinnamon, and sea salt. Serve hot.

For even more flavor, add coconut milk when mashing the potatoes. Excellent for breakfast too!

APPS

A mouth-watering introduction to dinner

Fresh Spring Rolls **264**

Sesame Tuna-Stuffed Mini Peppers **266**

Parmesan Crisps with Roasted Tomatoes **268**

Cucumber Hummus Boats **270**

Roasted Potato Bites
with Chive Parsley Tapenade **272**

Turkey-Sausage Stuffed Mushrooms **274**

Healthy Spinach Artichoke Dip **276**

Healthy Nachos **278**

FRESH SPRING ROLLS

MAKES ABOUT

12-15

THIN WRAPS

OR

10-12

THICK WRAPS

- 1 package rice paper wraps
- 2 large cucumbers, peeled and thinly sliced
- 3 carrots, thinly sliced
- 1 head romaine lettuce, each leaf sliced in half down the center
- 2 red bell peppers, sliced into matchsticks
- 15 leaves fresh mint, chopped
- 15 leaves fresh cilantro, chopped

DIRECTIONS

Grilled chicken, steak, cooked shrimp, hummus, or the **Peanut Sauce** would all be great additions to this basic recipe. I used a julienne slicer for the carrots and cucumber, but you can also cut them into matchsticks with a small knife, or use a regular vegetable peeler.

Fill a pie dish with water. Moisten a clean dish towel, and spread it out on the counter. Dip one rice paper wrap into the pan of water and submerge for 20-30 seconds. Remove and lay on the dishtowel.

Starting at one end of the wrap, add a romaine leaf. Cut away any ends that spill out. Add cucumber, carrot, and red bell peppers, layering them on top of each other in the romaine leaf. Tuck and roll the sides of the wrap with the veggies. Fold the bottom up, like a burrito, and continue to tuck and roll until the wrap is secure. Slice in half or thirds to store or serve.

Don't use too many ingredients, or the wraps will be very difficult to roll! These keep well in the fridge for up to 5 days. For a better visual, check out my YouTube how-to video for this recipe.

SESAME TUNA-STUFFED MINI PEPPERS

- 1/2 cup **Italian Tuna** Salad
- 5 assorted mini peppers
- \+ roasted sesame seeds for sprinkling

MAKES ABOUT 5 SERVINGS

A great make-ahead snack or party appetizer!

DIRECTIONS

Slice peppers in half, removing seeds and membranes. Scoop tuna into pepper halves and sprinkle with roasted sesame seeds to serve.

PARMESAN CRISPS with ROASTED TOMATOES

MAKES ABOUT 12 SERVINGS

- 2 cartons or 2 cups pre-shredded organic parmesan cheese
- 1 pint baby tomatoes, whole
- 2 teaspoons Italian seasoning (or dried basil and oregano)
- 1/2 teaspoon pepper
- 1/4 teaspoon sea salt

DIRECTIONS

- Roasted Tomatoes -

Preheat oven to 400°F. Line two baking sheets with parchment paper. Place tomatoes on one baking sheet, and drizzle with olive oil, sea salt, and pepper. Toss to coat, and place in the oven for 25 minutes or until slightly browned. When done, transfer to a bowl, add sea salt, pepper, and Italian seasoning and mash well with a fork. Set aside.

- Parmesan Crisps -

When ready to make the crisps, drop balls of grated parmesan cheese (about 1 tablespoon in size) into small mounds onto the second baking sheet. Place in oven at 400°F for approximately 6 minutes. Remove when the middle begins to brown like the edges. Transfer to the serving platter first. Spoon roasted tomato mixture over parmesan crisps to serve. Best when served hot.

This is hands down, my favorite party appetizer. It fills the house with the most amazing smell, and takes 6 minutes to make. You can easily roast the tomatoes ahead of time or use another topping you have on hand. The **Spring Pea + Mint Purée,** **Romesco Sauce,** *or* **Red Pepper Harissa Sauce,** *would all be awesome here!*

APPS

CUCUMBER HUMMUS BOATS

GF DF V

MAKES ABOUT 16 BITE SIZED-SERVINGS

- 4 cucumbers, peeled, sliced in half lengthwise with seeds scooped out
- 1 handful baby tomatoes, sliced in half lengthwise
- 1 container clean hummus
- 1 handful arugula (optional)

DIRECTIONS

Spread hummus in the middle of the cucumbers, where the seeds used to be. Top with tomatoes or other toppings. Sprinkle with sea salt and pepper, and slice into bite-sized pieces (or keep full sized for a bigger snack). Garnish with arugula.

If you don't like tomatoes, try adding fresh red peppers, avocado slices, or feta cheese on top for a great presentation. What qualifies as clean hummus? All ingredients you can recognize, and none that you can't!

ROASTED POTATO BITES
with CHIVE-PARSLEY TAPANADE

- 12 baby potatoes, halved, with rounded ends trimmed flat
- 1 .75 ounce container chives or ½ cup chopped
- 1 bunch fresh parsley, stems removed
- 2 cloves garlic
- 1/4 cup olive oil
- 1/2 teaspoon sea salt
- 1/2 teaspoon pepper

MAKES ABOUT 12 SERVINGS

DIRECTIONS

- Chive Parsley Tapanade -

Add all ingredients (except potatoes) to a blender with a splash or two of water. Blend until smooth, then transfer to a small ziplock plastic bag.

- Roasted Potato Bites -

Preheat the oven to 400°F. Line a baking sheet with parchment paper. Add potato halves and toss with olive oil. Sprinkle with sea salt and pepper. Bake for 30-35 minutes until brown, flipping halfway inbetween. Remove from heat and squeeze tapanade on top of each potato to serve by cutting a small corner off of the plastic sauce bag.

This fun appetizer is a riff on the classic baked-potato-with-sour-cream-and-onion combination. It can easily be prepped ahead of time and is a perfect one bite snack for entertaining. The tapenade freezes well, and works great as a marinade for meat, fish, and veggies.

TURKEY-SAUSAGE STUFFED MUSHROOMS

MAKES ABOUT 26 MUSHROOM BITES

- **26** large white or cremini mushrooms, stems separated and chopped
- **1** pound organic ground turkey, pork, chicken, or beef
- **1** granny smith apple, finely chopped
- **1/2** yellow or sweet onion, chopped
- **1/4** cup parmesan cheese
- **5** ounces goat cheese (approximately ¼ cup)
- **2** teaspoons fennel seeds
- **1** teaspoon fresh sage or 3 teaspoons dried sage
- **1** teaspoon pepper
- **1/2** teaspoon sea salt

DIRECTIONS

Pre-heat oven to 350°F. Line a baking sheet with parchment paper.

Wash each mushroom, then wipe dry with a paper towel. Add mushroom caps to the baking sheet, top-side down. Rub each mushroom with a bit of olive oil. Sprinkle with sea salt and pepper, and bake in the oven for 10-15 minutes.

In the meantime, add a tablespoon of olive oil to a skillet over medium heat. Add onion and apple, and sauté for a few minutes. Add chopped mushroom stems to the pan. Cook for a few minutes, then set aside in a mixing bowl. Add both cheeses to the bowl, and stir well to combine.

Add ground turkey to the skillet. Break up with a fork, and let all sides cook evenly. Add fennel seeds, sage, sea salt, and pepper. When fully cooked, add the turkey to the other ingredients in the mixing bowl. Stir well.

Remove mushroom heads from the oven and drain any excess water out of the middles. Turn up the heat to 400°F. Stuff the mushrooms with the turkey mixture and place back in the oven for another 10 minutes or until they begin to brown. Serve warm.

Buy the biggest mushrooms you can find for this recipe—they shrink like crazy when they're cooked. For an extra delicious twist, try adding some extra grated parmesan, gouda, or sharp cheddar cheese; or use quinoa or brown rice instead of meat; or, if you don't like mushrooms, use tomatoes or bell peppers instead.

HEALTHY SPINACH ARTICHOKE DIP

MAKES ABOUT **10** SERVINGS

- 1   16 ounce bag frozen organic spinach
- 1   can artichoke hearts, rinsed, drained, and quartered
- 1   cup whole milk greek yogurt
- 1/2 onion, roughly chopped
- 2   cloves garlic
- 1   teaspoon sea salt
- 1   teaspoon pepper

DIRECTIONS

Preheat oven to 375°F. In a blender, combine spinach, artichokes, yogurt, onion, and garlic. Add a tiny bit of water so you can blend the mixture easily. Once combined, generously season with sea salt and pepper, and pour into a shallow baking dish. Bake for 35 minutes or until it starts to brown around the edges. Optional to add cheese over the top and broil on high for a few minutes before serving. Serve warm.

This dip is amazing on a crudité platter with carrots, celery, cucumbers, radishes, organic corn chips or toast of your choice. Also optional to add gorgonzola, parmesan, cheddar, or gruyere cheese on top, and broil before serving.

APPS

HEALTHY NACHOS

- **1** bag organic corn chips
- **1** grilled and sliced chicken breast (or ½ cup cooked ground chicken, turkey, pork, or beef) (optional)
- **1** can refried beans
- **1** bunch radishes, sliced
- **1** jalapeño, sliced into rounds
- **1/2** cup parmesan cheese, grated
- **1/4** cup crumbled feta cheese

MAKES ABOUT

SERVINGS

DIRECTIONS

Preheat oven to 400°F. Line a baking sheet with parchment paper. Spread organic corn chips in a single layer on the sheet. Add a bit of refried beans to most chips with a spoon. Add chicken or meat, sprinkle with parmesan cheese, and add jalapeños on top. Bake for 10-15 minutes or until the cheese melts. Remove from oven; sprinkle with feta cheese, radishes, and cilantro to serve.

Mashed avocado or guacamole, salsa, whole milk sour cream or greek yogurt, and chopped cilantro all make excellent garnishes for serving.

EVERYDAY

SNACKS

Healthy Party Mix **282**
Curry Roasted Cashews **284**
Coconut Oil Popcorn **286**
Spiced Sweet Potato Chips **290**
Maple Pecans **292**

Because most snacks are full of junk, here's how to do them the real food way. All are great for daily life or entertaining.

HEALTHY PARTY MIX

MAKES ABOUT

12

SERVINGS

- 6 cups square rice cereal
- 1 cup raw or dry roasted peanuts
- 1/2 cup raw or dry roasted sunflower seeds
- 3 tablespoons coconut oil
- 1 teaspoon gluten free fish sauce
- 1/2 teaspoon toasted sesame oil
- 1/4 teaspoon garlic powder
- 1/4 teaspoon onion powder

For best results, store this party mix in a glass container in the fridge for up to 2 weeks. To keep it gluten free, choose a cereal brand that uses only rice or rice and corn.

DIRECTIONS

Preheat oven to 375°F, and line a baking sheet with parchment paper. Add rice cereal, peanuts, and sunflower seeds to a mixing bowl. Melt the coconut oil in a separate bowl and add the fish sauce, toasted sesame oil, garlic, and onion powder. Gently pour the warm mixture over the dry cereal mix. Toss gently with your hands to coat. Spread the mixture evenly on the baking sheet and toast for 10-15 minutes until slightly brown and crisp.

SNACKS

CURRY COCONUT CASHEWS

1	cup raw cashews
1	cup large coconut flakes
1	tablespoon coconut oil
1	teaspoon curry powder
1/2	teaspoon cinnamon
1/4	teaspoon garlic powder
1/4	teaspoon sea salt

MAKES ABOUT 4 SERVINGS

DIRECTIONS

Preheat oven to 350°F and line a baking sheet with parchment paper. Add cashews and coconut flakes to a medium mixing bowl. In a small saucepan over low heat, combine coconut oil and spices. When warm and liquefied, pour over the nuts and toss to coat. Distribute evenly onto the baking sheet, and roast for 10-12 minutes, stirring occasionally until they are slightly brown on top.

Another great snack for any occasion. These nuts will keep fresh in a sealed container for up to 1 week.

This recipe is amazing on its own, or as a base for other favorite toppings of your choice: parmesan cheese and black pepper; melted caramel sauce; melted honey; peanut butter and raisins; or chopped herbs and butter. If you love popcorn, get yourself a Whirly Pop™—it's the best popcorn maker! Check out the resources page on my website to get a direct link to the one I love and use the most.

SNACKS

COCONUT OIL POPCORN

- **1/2** cup organic popcorn kernels
- **1** tablespoon unrefined coconut oil + 2 tablespoons for melting
- **1/2** teaspoon sea salt

MAKES ABOUT

4

SERVINGS

DIRECTIONS

Heat 1 tablespoon of coconut oil in a large stock pot with lid, or use a Whirly Pop™. Pour in kernels and cover. When you start to hear some popping, shake the pot around or spin your Whirly Pop™ until the popping slows. Dump into a large mixing bowl. Place the pot back on the stove and add 2 tablespoons of coconut oil. When melted, drizzle over the popcorn, toss to coat the kernels evenly, and sprinkle with sea salt to serve.

> EXPERIENCING MORE JOY WITH FOOD IS HUGE. YOU COULD EAT PERFECTLY, BUT IF YOU'RE ALL WOUND UP IN YOUR HEAD WITH GUILT OR OBSESSIONS, YOU WON'T AND CAN'T DIGEST IT WELL. BE HEALTHY IN YOUR THOUGHTS, ACTIONS AND FOOD—IT ALL GOES TOGETHER.

SPICED SWEET POTATO CHIPS

MAKES ABOUT **6** SERVINGS

- 2 thin sweet potatoes or yams, sliced as thin as you can get them
- 1 1/2 tablespoons melted coconut oil
- 1 teaspoon cinnamon
- 1 teaspoon cumin
- 1/2 teaspoon sea salt

DIRECTIONS

Preheat oven to 300°F. Line a baking sheet with parchment paper. Add sliced yams to the baking sheet. In a separate saucepan, add coconut oil, cinnamon, cumin and sea salt and stir until the oil melts. Pour the oil over the chips and rub each yam with your fingers to coat. Place in the oven to bake for 15-20 minutes, watching them carefully.

A mandoline slicer or sharp knife (and steady knife skills) is key to getting thin chips that will crisp up in the oven. Store in an airtight container for up to 5 days.

SPICED MAPLE PECANS

2	cups pecans
2	tablespoons coconut oil
1	tablespoon maple syrup
1	teaspoon cinnamon
1/4	teaspoon cayenne pepper
1/4	teaspoon sea salt

MAKES ABOUT

6

SERVINGS

DIRECTIONS

Preheat oven to 350°F and line a baking sheet with parchment paper. Melt the coconut oil and maple syrup together first. Stir in cinnamon, cayenne and sea salt and mix well to combine. Add pecans to a mixing bowl and pour the coconut oil mixture in. Stir well. Spread nuts on the baking sheet and bake for 10-12 minutes or until they start to brown.

These are the perfect slightly spicy and slightly sweet crunchy snack. They're also great as a topping for salads and when paired with **Coconut Mashed Yams.**

DRESSINGS AND SAUCES

- Easy Everyday Balsamic **296**
- Roasted Red Pepper Harissa Sauce **298**
- Cucumber Yogurt Dressing **300**
- Green Goddess Dressing **302**
- Romesco Sauce **304**
- Spring Pea + Mint Purée **306**
- Cilantro Avocado Dressing **308**
- Honey Mustard Poppy Seed Dressing **310**
- Mango Jalapeño Pineapple Salsa **312**
- Cilantro, Lime + Ginger Marinade **314**
- Mediterranean Lemon Tahini Dressing **316**
- Herbed Chimichurri **318**
- Peanut Sauce **320**
- Cherry Balsamic Sauce **322**
- Sweet Apple + Cranberry Sauce **324**
- Coconut Whipped Cream **326**

DRESSINGS + SAUCES

EASY EVERYDAY BALSAMIC

- **4** tablespoons olive oil
- **2** tablespoons balsamic vinegar
- **1** tablespoon dijon mustard
- **+** sea salt and pepper to taste

MAKES ABOUT

2

SERVINGS

DIRECTIONS

Combine all ingredients in a bowl or jar and whisk or shake to blend.

Never buy pre-made dressing again! This basic version can be tinkered with by adding extra herbs or chopped garlic and onion, or by swapping out types of vinegar. Store in a sealed container in the fridge for up to 1 week.

ROASTED RED PEPPER HARISSA

MAKES ABOUT

4

SERVINGS

- 2 red bell peppers, sliced into equal-sized pieces
- 1 jalapeño pepper, sliced in half
- 1 pint baby tomatoes (approximately 2 cups)
- 1 clove garlic, peeled
- 3 teaspoons cumin
- 1/2 teaspoon pepper
- 1/4 teaspoon sea salt

DIRECTIONS

Preheat oven to 400°F. On a baking sheet lined with parchment paper, spread out the sliced peppers, jalapeño, garlic, and whole tomatoes. Drizzle all with a bit of olive oil, sea salt, and pepper. Roast for 20-25 minutes or until the veggies char a bit. Let cool, then place all ingredients in a blender with some water (adding just enough so that it can blend smoothly), cumin, and a big splash of olive oil. This sauce freezes well if you have any leftover.

*This sauce is the perfect little addition to chicken, other types of meat, fish, veggies, brown rice, quinoa, **Baked Spaghetti Squash**, **Mini Sliders**, or **Organic Greek Meatballs**. Or, my favorite: straight from the fridge with a spoon.*

CUCUMBER YOGURT DRESSING

MAKES ABOUT 8 SERVINGS

- 1 cup organic whole milk greek yogurt
- 1 cucumber or ½ English cucumber, seeds scooped out and thinly sliced
- 1 tablespoon fresh dill, chopped or 3 teaspoons dried
- 1 tablespoon fresh mint, chopped
- 1 teaspoon lemon juice
- 1 clove garlic, chopped
- + sea salt and pepper to taste

DIRECTIONS

Combine all ingredients in a bowl and stir together.

*This dressing pairs perfectly with the **Mini Falafel Balls**, **Falafel Salad**, the **Chopped Greek Salad**, **Mini Sliders**, or **Molasses Ginger Salmon**. Keeps great in the fridge for up to 1 week.*

DRESSINGS + SAUCES

GREEN GODDESS DRESSING

1/2	avocado
5	tablespoons olive oil
10	leaves basil
1	lemon, juiced
1	teaspoon anchovy paste
1	handful chopped chives (approximately 6 sprigs chopped)
+	sea salt and pepper to taste

MAKES ABOUT

4

SERVINGS

DIRECTIONS

Blend all ingredients together in a blender or food processor. Add more olive oil if you prefer a thinner consistency. Store in the fridge for up to 1 week.

This is a great creamy but non-dairy dressing for any salad, marinade for any meat or fish, and dip for a crudité platter.

ROMESCO SAUCE

MAKES ABOUT 6 SERVINGS

- 2 red bell peppers
- 2 cloves garlic
- 6 tablespoons almonds
- 5 tablespoons olive oil
- 2 teaspoons sherry vinegar
- 2 teaspoons smoked paprika
- 1 teaspoon pepper
- 1/2 teaspoon sea salt

DIRECTIONS

Preheat oven to 400°F. Slice bell peppers into equal-sized chunks, and spread out on a parchment-lined baking sheet. Add garlic cloves to baking sheet as well. Drizzle all with olive oil and sprinkle with sea salt and pepper. Roast for 15 minutes or until the peppers start to wrinkle. Remove and let cool. In a blender, combine olive oil, vinegar, and almonds; blend these first, adding a bit of water if necessary. Then, add the roasted peppers, garlic, sea salt and pepper and blend until smooth.

This Spanish-influenced recipe is one of my favorites any time of year. It's another perfectly versatile sauce for chicken, steak, shrimp, fish, veggies, egg dishes, potatoes, or rice. Any leftover sauce freezes beautifully.

SPRING PEA + MINT PURÉE

1	16 ounce package frozen peas
10	large leaves fresh mint
1/2	onion, roughly chopped
1/2	cup shredded parmesan cheese
4	tablespoons organic melted butter or olive oil
1	clove garlic
1	teaspoon pepper
1/4	teaspoon sea salt

MAKES ABOUT

SERVINGS

Great over potatoes, grilled fish, meat, or veggies; even better straight up by the spoonful!

DIRECTIONS

Add peas, onion, and garlic to a saucepan with enough water to cover and bring to a boil. Cook according to the pea package, approximately 5-7 minutes. Drain when ready. Add peas, onion, and garlic to a blender with melted butter or olive oil, mint, sea salt, and pepper. Add a tiny bit of water or olive oil if needed to blend. Blend until smooth.

CILANTRO AVOCADO DRESSING

MAKES ABOUT **6** SERVINGS

- 2 limes, juiced (approximately 6 tablespoons)
- 1 jalapeño pepper, de-seeded and chopped
- 1 clove garlic
- 1/2 avocado, pitted
- 1/2 cup cilantro leaves, chopped
- 6 tablespoons extra-virgin olive oil
- 1/2 teaspoon pepper
- 1/4 teaspoon sea salt

This dressing is perfect on tacos and salads, or as a marinade for meat or fish. Store in a small glass jar in the fridge for up to 1 week.

DIRECTIONS

Add all ingredients together in a blender to combine. Add more olive oil and lime juice if you prefer a thinner consistency.

DRESSINGS + SAUCES

HONEY MUSTARD POPPY SEED DRESSING

- **5** tablespoons olive oil
- **3** tablespoons raw apple cider vinegar
- **2** tablespoons honey
- **2** tablespoons dijon mustard
- **2** teaspoons poppy seeds
- **+** sea salt and pepper to taste

MAKES ABOUT

SERVINGS

DIRECTIONS

Combine all ingredients in a blender. Blend until smooth.

This dressing is great for salads or veggies, or for marinating chicken! Keeps well in the fridge for up to 1 week.

MANGO JALAPEÑO PINEAPPLE SALSA

MAKES ABOUT 8 SERVINGS

- 5 mangos, peeled and cut into bite-sized cubes (approximately 4 cups)
- 1 fresh pineapple, cut into bite-sized cubes (approximately 3 cups)
- 2-3 jalapeños, seeded and chopped
- 1/2 red onion, thinly sliced and chopped
- 1/2 cup cilantro, chopped

Serve over grilled fish or chicken, or as a salsa with organic corn chips. Or for homemade ceviche. Keeps fresh for up to 3 days in the fridge.

DIRECTIONS

Combine all ingredients in a bowl, sprinkle with sea salt and pepper and cover. Chill for a least 1 hour before serving, if possible, to let the flavors mix together.

DRESSINGS + SAUCES

DRESSINGS + SAUCES

CILANTRO, LIME + GINGER MARINADE

2-3	limes, juiced (approximately ¼ cup)
1/2	cup olive oil
2	tablespoons tamari sauce
2	teaspoons cilantro, chopped
1	teaspoon unrefined toasted sesame oil
1	teaspoon fresh ginger, grated
1	teaspoon honey
+	sea salt and pepper to taste

MAKES ABOUT

SERVINGS

A perfect pairing for salads, or as a marinade for meat or seafood.

DIRECTIONS

Combine all ingredients together in a blender. Blend until smooth.

MEDITERRANEAN LEMON TAHINI DRESSING

MAKES ABOUT

6

SERVINGS

- 1/3 cup extra-virgin olive oil
- 1 tablespoon tahini
- 2 cloves garlic, pressed or chopped
- 1 lemon, juiced (approximately ¼ cup)
- 2 teaspoons honey
- + sea salt and pepper to taste

DIRECTIONS

Combine all ingredients together in a blender. Blend until smooth.

DRESSINGS + SAUCES

This dressing is a great marinade for meat or seafood, and a fun tangy salad dressing or vegetable dip. Keeps well in the fridge for up to 7 days.

HERBED CHIMICHURRI

- **1** bunch parsley (approximately 1 cup), leaves only
- **1** bunch cilantro (approximately 1 cup), leaves only
- **3** tablespoons capers
- **2** cloves garlic
- **1/2** cup olive oil
- **1 1/2** tablespoons white wine vinegar
- **1/2** teaspoon red pepper flakes
- **1/2** teaspoon ground black pepper
- **1/2** teaspoons sea salt

MAKES ABOUT

6

SERVINGS

DIRECTIONS

For a traditional chimichurri sauce, chop all ingredients finely and mix with olive oil. If you are short on time, add all ingredients to a blender and blend to your desired consistency.

Perfect for steak, chicken, grilled veggies, or as a salad dressing. Leftover sauce can be frozen in silicone ice cube trays for easy single-serving use.

PEANUT SAUCE

1. 16 ounce can of coconut milk
2. tablespoons tamari sauce (gf) or shoyu sauce
4. tablespoons natural peanut butter, almond butter, or tahini
2. tablespoons honey

+ sprinkle of cayenne pepper
+ sprinkle of sea salt

MAKES ABOUT

8

SERVINGS

DIRECTIONS

Whisk all ingredients together in a saucepan over low heat until warm.

*The perfect addition to the **Larb Lettuce Wraps, Fresh Spring Rolls**, stir-fries, or grilled chicken or vegetables.*

CHERRY BALSAMIC SAUCE

1/2	cup pitted cherries (frozen and defrosted are fine)
6	tablespoons balsamic vinegar
2	tablespoons olive oil
2	cloves garlic
1	teaspoon pure maple syrup
1	teaspoon dijon mustard
+	sea salt and pepper to taste

MAKES ABOUT

SERVINGS

DIRECTIONS

Combine all ingredients in a blender. Blend until mostly smooth.

*This is a great sauce to make a double batch of and use on other roasted veggies, in quinoa, millet, brown rice, over meat or fish or even on ice cream! Or try the **Cherry Balsamic Roasted Chicken** recipe.*

SWEET APPLE + CRANBERRY SAUCE

MAKES ABOUT

CUPS

- 12 cups fresh cranberries (approximately 5 bags)
- 12 dates, pits removed and chopped
- 2 sweet apples, chopped
- 3 fresh cinnamon sticks
- 1 1/2 cups water
- + sea salt to taste

DIRECTIONS

In a large soup pot over high heat, add cranberries, water, and a few dashes of sea salt. Cover, and bring to a boil. Once boiling, stir berries, and reduce heat to medium-low. Cover and cook for about 10 minutes. Add dates, apples, and cinnamon sticks to the cranberry mixture. Cook until apples are softened through, approximately 10-15 minutes. Depending on your preferences, leave the sauce as is or remove cinnamon sticks and blend with an immersion blender for a smoother texture. Optional to add 1-2 tablespoons of honey or maple syrup if you prefer a sweeter sauce.

DRESSINGS + SAUCES

I promise you—canned cranberry sauce will be a thing of the past after you try this recipe. Sweeter varieties of apples to use include Gala, Red Delicious, Honeycrisp or Fuji.

COCONUT WHIPPED CREAM

MAKES ABOUT 4 SERVINGS

- **1** 16 ounce can of regular coconut milk
- **1** teaspoon vanilla

DIRECTIONS

Place a can of coconut milk upside down in the fridge for 2 hours. Flip right-side up and open, scooping the thick part of the mixture into a blender. Leave the water behind (side note: save it to use it in smoothies, coffee, or iced tea). Add 1 teaspoon vanilla to the blender and blend on very low speed for a minute until whipped.

*Serve chilled with berries of your choice, or on top of cooked **Apple Cinnamon Morning Quinoa, Two Ingredient Pancakes** or other desserts! Use regular canned coconut in this recipe, not the light version.*

SPECIALTY COCKTAILS

Aperol Spritz **330**

Prosecco + St Germaine with Strawberries **332**

Cucumber Basil Gin + Tonics **334**

Sage Gin Fizz **336**

Sarah's Classic Healthy Margarita **338**

Fresh Grapefruit Greyhound **342**

Chai-Infused Whiskey **344**

When well made, a cocktail is a work of art and one of the best parts of a healthy lifestyle because of what comes with it—slowing down, being in the moment, talking and connecting to those you love over great food. There is nothing I love more. These versions are some of my favorites, with all the good stuff and none of the extra sugary syrups or chemicals than sometime sneak into more traditional recipes. All you'll need is some club soda, good quality liquors, and some fresh juices or fruit.

APEROL SPRITZ

- **6** ounces club soda or prosecco
- **3** ounces high quality vodka or gin
- **1 1/2** ounces Aperol

MAKES ABOUT 2 SERVINGS

DIRECTIONS

Stir all ingredients together and pour into two wine glasses filled with ice. Garnish with an orange peel, orange slice, or wedge of lime.

This recipe is a well know Italian aperitif, and one of my very favorites. If you're not familiar with Aperol, it's a beautiful bitter with great digestive properties. It definitely deserves a spot in your home cocktail bar.

PROSECCO + ST GERMAINE *with* STRAWBERRIES

MAKES ABOUT

2

SERVINGS

- **6** ounces prosecco, chilled
- **2** ounces St. Germaine
- **2** strawberries

DIRECTIONS

Pour prosecco and St. Germaine into chilled champagne flutes. Add a strawberry to each glass to serve.

Chilled prosecco gets a great upgrade in this recipe with the addition of St. Germaine. This recipe also works well with Campari or Aperol instead of St. Germaine, or by swapping out the strawberries for any seasonal fruit.

CUCUMBER BASIL GIN + TONICS

MAKES ABOUT

2

SERVINGS

- **6** ounces club soda
- **3** ounces high-quality gin
- **3** ounces natural tonic water
- **1** lime, juiced
- **4** large basil leaves
- **1/4** cucumber, sliced

For best results, use a natural tonic water (one with no high fructose corn syrup). Feel free to change the herbs and garnishes in this drink to whatever is in season or already in your fridge.

DIRECTIONS

Muddle basil, lime juice, and gin in a glass or cocktail shaker. Add cucumber slices, club soda and tonic. Pour over ice to serve and garnish with extra lime wedges.

SPECIALTY COCKTAILS

SAGE GIN FIZZ

SAGE GIN FIZZ

- 4-6 sage leaves
- 3 ounces high quality gin
- 3 ounces club soda
- 2 ounces honey, molasses, maple syrup, or homemade simple syrup

HOMEMADE HEALTHY SIMPLE SYRUP

- 6 teaspoons honey, maple syrup or molasses
- 1/2 cup water

MAKES ABOUT

2

SERVINGS

DIRECTIONS

Muddle sage leaves with gin and a splash of the **Homemade Simple Syrup** or other natural sweetener. Pour over ice, and add club soda. Stir. Garnish with extra sage.

- Homemade Healthy Simple Syrup -

Unlike traditional simple syrup, this upgrade uses natural sweeteners instead of white sugar—leading to less of a blood sugar spike when ingested. Honey will have the lightest and most neutral taste, while molasses usually pairs best with heavier whiskey or bourbon-based cocktails.

Add natural sweetener of your choice and ½ cup water to a small saucepan on low heat. Stir until the sweetener dissolves. Let cool before adding to cocktails. You'll only need a splash for most cocktails that have bitter flavors that need rounding out. Dilute the mixture as needed. Store in a sealed container in the fridge for up to a week.

If you don't have time to make your own syrup, use a splash of Cointreau, St. Germaine, or prosecco instead.

SPECIALTY COCKTAILS

SARAH'S CLASSIC HEALTHY MARGARITA

- **6** ounces club soda
- **3** ounces high quality tequila
- **2** limes, juiced
- **2** splashes of Cointreau

MAKES ABOUT

2

SERVINGS

DIRECTIONS

Split ingredients between two glasses adding in this order: club soda, tequila, lime juice then Cointreau. Stir well. Add ice and extra limes wedges to serve.

This recipe is one of my favorite cocktails for any time of year. It can also be easily tweaked to add other fun flavors: try muddled blackberries, infused jalapeño tequila, lemons instead of limes, or a splash of ginger kombucha or fresh-pressed beet juice. Garnish with extra lime wedges or wheels.

> "I LOVE A GREAT COCKTAIL. AND WINE. AND DESSERT. I WOULD NEVER WANT TO LIVE A LIFE THAT DIDN'T INVOLVE THESE THINGS (WITHOUT GUILT).

FRESH GRAPEFRUIT GREYHOUND

MAKES ABOUT

2

SERVINGS

- **6** ounces club soda
- **3** ounces high quality vodka
- **1** grapefruit juiced (approximately 6 ounces)

DIRECTIONS

Split ingredients between two glasses with ice. Stir well and serve.

SPECIALTY COCKTAILS

Also great made with fresh orange or lemon juice. Garnish with extra grapefruit slices to serve.

SPECIALTY COCKTAILS

CHAI-INFUSED WHISKEY

- **3** ounces whiskey
- **3** teaspoons raw honey or maple syrup
- **2** chai tea bags
- **2** cinnamon sticks for garnish
- **1** orange, sliced

MAKES ABOUT

2

SERVINGS

DIRECTIONS

Boil 1 cup water with 2 chai tea bags. Let steep for a few minutes, add honey until it dissolves, and cool to room temperature (or place in the fridge). Add tea mixture and whiskey to two glasses with ice. Garnish with orange wheels and cinnamon sticks.

This recipe is great with or without the sweetener added, and can be made with other kinds of tea as well. Serve in a short or old-fashioned style glass with ice, or serve hot in mugs!

DESSERTS

Sarah's Best Chocolate Chip Cookies **348**

Pistachio + Chocolate Covered Frozen Bananas **350**

Strawberry Rhubarb Crisp **352**

Sarah's Peanut Butter Cookies **354**

Mini Coconut Almond Macaroons **356**

Granola Bar Bites **358**

Homemade Ice Cream Cake with Cookie Crunch **360**

Molten Chocolate Olive Oil Cake **362**

What qualifies as a "healthy" dessert? One made with real food ingredients of course. With real butter, eggs (or chia seeds) and dark chocolate. All of the following recipes are gluten free by nature using some alternative flours, but without losing any of the great tastes and textures. And with natural sugars whenever possible. So you can have all the sweet parts of life without compromising feeling great.

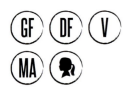

SARAH'S BEST CHOCOLATE CHIP COOKIES

MAKES ABOUT

12

COOKIES

- 1 cup almond meal or gluten free flour
- 1 dark chocolate bar, chopped finely or ½ cup dark chocolate chips
- 3/4 cup sugar or coconut sugar
- 4 tablespoons hazelnut milk
- 4 tablespoons coconut oil, melted
- 1 tablespoon chia seeds
- 1 teaspoon vanilla
- + dash of sea salt

For a thin and crunchy cookie, use almond meal in this recipe. For a more traditional and softer cookie, use a gluten free flour blend.

DIRECTIONS

First combine chia seeds and 3 tablespoons water in a small dish and let sit while you prep the rest of the ingredients. Preheat oven to 350°F and line a baking sheet with parchment paper. Combine all ingredients in a mixing bowl. Add chia seed paste, and mix to combine. Add teaspoon-sized drops of batter on the baking sheet, making sure to leave enough space between them—these spread fast as they bake. Bake for 10-15 minutes, depending on how crunchy you like your cookies.

DESSERTS

PISTACHIO + CHOCOLATE COVERED FROZEN BANANAS

MAKES ABOUT

12-15

BITES

- 2 bananas, sliced into 1 inch pieces
- 1 dark chocolate bar
- 1/4 cup pistachios, shelled and chopped
- + sea salt for sprinkling

DIRECTIONS

In a saucepan, melt chocolate on low heat, stirring frequently. Set aside. Dip banana pieces in melted chocolate (one side only) and place, chocolate-side up, on parchment paper. Sprinkle with chopped pistachios then sprinkle with sea salt. Freeze for at least 1 hour before serving.

Try dipping these sweet healthy bites in shredded coconut or peanut butter too! You can swap out the type of nut as well, depending on what you have in your pantry.

STRAWBERRY RHUBARB CRISP

- 8 cups quartered strawberries
- 2 cups chopped rhubarb (approximately 3 stalks)
- 1 cup gluten free flour blend
- 1 cup gluten free oats
- 5 tablespoons butter or coconut oil, melted
- 1 tablespoon honey or maple syrup
- 2 teaspoons cinnamon
- 1 teaspoon vanilla extract
- 1/2 teaspoon sea salt

DIRECTIONS

Preheat oven to 375°F. Spray a rectangular baking dish with some coconut or olive oil. Add strawberries and rhubarb to the bottom of the baking dish. In a small bowl, melt the butter or coconut oil.

In a separate mixing bowl, combine the flour, oats, and spices. Pour melted butter or coconut oil into the mixing bowl and crumble the mixture with your hands. Spread mixture evenly over the top of the strawberries and rhubarb.

Cover crisp, and bake for 25-30 minutes. Remove cover and bake until the top browns and the fruit bubbles up, approximately 10 minutes more.

The fruit filling in this recipe can be varied depending on the season. I've made it with peaches, plums, apples, pears, or all types of berries. But this combo below is my favorite. Perfect served with vanilla or coconut milk ice cream or homemade **Coconut Whipped Cream.**

SARAH'S PEANUT BUTTER COOKIES

MAKES ABOUT
30
BITE-SIZED COOKIES

- 1 cup chunky or smooth peanut butter or almond butter
- 1/2 cup honey
- 1/4 cup maple syrup
- 1 egg
- 3 tablespoons chopped dark chocolate or dark chocolate chips (optional)
- 3 teaspoons chia seeds
- 1/2 teaspoon sea salt

These sweet cookies are great made with smooth or chunky peanut or almond butter. Or, you can add a tiny scoop of vanilla or chocolate ice cream in between two cookies for the cutest ice cream sandwich bites you've ever seen!

DIRECTIONS

Preheat oven to 350°F and line two baking sheets with parchment paper. In a mixing bowl, combine peanut butter, egg, honey, and maple syrup. Add chocolate pieces, if using, and sea salt. Mix well and refrigerate for 10 minutes. Remove batter and drop teaspoon-sized balls onto the baking sheet, using your fingers to form a chocolate kiss shape. Pat middle peak down softly with the pads of your fingers. Lightly cross each cookie with fork tines to make a crisscross pattern. Bake for 15 minutes or until browned on top.

DESSERTS

MINI COCONUT ALMOND MACAROONS

MAKES ABOUT 30 MINI COOKIES

- 4 cups shredded coconut
- 4 egg whites
- 1/2 cup slivered almonds, chopped finely
- 1/4 cup honey, melted
- 3 tablespoons coconut oil, melted
- 2 teaspoons vanilla extract
- 1/4 teaspoon sea salt

Warning: These are slightly addicting. And just the perfect amount of "a little something sweet" when you need it.

DIRECTIONS

Preheat oven to 350°F. Line two baking sheets with parchment paper. In a bowl, whisk egg whites, honey and coconut oil together. Add the coconut, chopped slivered almonds, vanilla, and sea salt, and stir to combine. Form small balls with your hands, squeezing out any excess liquid as you go, and arrange on the baking sheet. Bake for 22-24 minutes or until slightly golden brown.

DESSERTS

GRANOLA BAR BITES

1/2	cup natural nut butter
1/4	cup maple syrup or honey
1	cup unsweetened coconut
1	cup gluten free oats
1	teaspoon vanilla
+	sprinkle of sea salt
+	small handful of dark chocolate chips, raisins, chopped nuts, or other dried fruit (optional)

MAKES ABOUT 24 COOKIE BITES

Feel free to use almond, peanut, or sunflower-seed butter interchangeably. Kid approved too!

DIRECTIONS

Mix all ingredients together in a large bowl, and place in fridge for at least 30 minutes. Scoop out 1 inch balls with a spoon, and arrange on a baking sheet or plate. Store in the fridge or freezer.

DESSERTS

HOMEMADE ICE CREAM CAKE *with* COOKIE CRUNCH

MAKES ABOUT

8-10

SERVINGS

- **1** large carton of your favorite ice cream
- **1** large carton of your second-favorite ice cream
- **2** boxes of graham or animal crackers (gf brand), crushed

DIRECTIONS

Take ice cream out of the freezer and let sit for 5-10 minutes. Line matching pie or cake pans with plastic wrap, leaving a bit of an overhang on all sides. When ice cream is soft enough, scoop out each flavor and mash them into separate pie pans, smoothing the top with the back of a spoon.

Sprinkle a thick layer of crushed graham or animal crackers on top of whatever flavor you want to be the top layer of the cake. Then cover the top of both pans in plastic wrap, and re-freeze for at least 2 hours.

When ready to assemble, unwrap the ice cream pan without the cracker crumble and flip on to a serving plate. Add the second ice cream cake on top so the crumble topping is in the middle. Store in the freezer until ready to serve.

You will need two matching glass or aluminum pie pans. Fun garnishes could include berries, cherries, chocolate sauce, or chopped mint.

MOLTEN CHOCOLATE OLIVE OIL CAKE

- 1 1/2 cups almond flour or almond meal
- 2/3 cup olive oil
- 2 eggs
- 1 cup sugar
- 6 tablespoons unsweetened cocoa powder
- 1/2 cup boiling water
- 2 teaspoons vanilla extract
- 1/2 teaspoon baking soda
- 1/4 teaspoon sea salt

MAKES ABOUT 12 SERVINGS

DIRECTIONS

Preheat oven to 325°F. Line a pie pan with parchment paper.

In a medium bowl, combine cocoa powder, sugar, vanilla, and boiling water. Whisk to combine. Then, add olive oil and eggs to the chocolate mixture, and whisk together. In a different bowl, combine almond flour, baking soda, and sea salt. Pour dry ingredients into the chocolate mixture, and stir well to make batter.

Pour batter into a parchment-lined pie pan (trimming edges down) and bake for 45 minutes for a gooey inside, or 50 minutes for a more cake-like texture.

Serve with fresh strawberries and chopped mint, sliced figs, coconut milk ice cream, ice cream or **Coconut Whipped Cream.**

EXTRA LOVE + THANK YOUS

MOM—My cookbook angel. Without you, this cookbook would not have been possible. Literally. Thank you for your weekly help shopping, cooking, and endless chopping on some of the most beautiful summer days. For giving up your time and giving me so much extra love every single week. Your presence soothed me, encouraged me, and kept me grounded through the entire process, just as it does in the rest of my life.

DAD—Here it is. "The book"! The one you've been telling me for years to write. This one is for you. Thank you for always encouraging my passion for all things healthy from the age of 7 on, and for being my #1 fan, everyday of my life.

LAUREN—My filter. Counterpart. Roommate. Bestie. Life partner. In-house editor. Thank you for keeping me sane, for editing this entire book, line by line, for wiping my tears and coming to the rescue each and every time I wanted to stop. Thank you for the fierceness of your love and the contagious energy that you bring to my life on the daily.

KYLE—To my #1 recipe tester, permanent dish washer, encourager and supporter. For making me laugh, keeping me calm, and inspiring me to be the best and truest version of myself. You light up my life and bring me so much joy.

KRISTIN—Thank you for taking my dreams and visions and turning them into this beautiful masterpiece that you're holding. Your stunning amount of patience, love, late nights, and amazing talent shine throughout this whole book. You are such a blessing to me, my business, and my life! Project cookbook, done. And it is beyond my wildest dreams.

JASMINE—My partner in crime on the craziest part of this project of mine. Since day one in that crowded little coffee shop, this book is a reality because of your hard work and amazing effort. We did it! Thank you for your candor and creativity, for forcing me to push the lines and for turning my recipes into beautiful works of art to share with the world. You are a blessing.

NICK—For editing this entire book. For giving your time, your energy, and your amazing input. Your attention to detail and care was a godsend. Thank you for everything you have done to make this book possible!

KERI- For also editing this entire book. Your timing was impeccable, as were your comments and wise advice. I must have learned from the best!

BRIAN- Thank you for coming to the rescue with such insightful and timely help in the editing process.

EDWARD + NANCY OF STARKMAN PRINTERS—Thank you for your speedy help, wise words, and incredible work in facilitating the printing of this book—my baby—and putting your care and love into each and every step.

WEST ELM SEATTLE—Your generosity and support of this project has been incredible and I feel so thankful for companies like yours that love and support their community. So many of the dishes and beautiful props that you see in this book are from the West Elm Seattle store. Thank you, thank you!

CLIENTS + BLOG READERS—For you, this is all for you.

For recipe testing and giving me your feedback, for letting me into your lives and your kitchens, and the stories that they bring. Thank you for every email, every post, every text, every comment throughout this whole process, and throughout the evolution of Simply Real Health. You guys encourage me to keep going, even on the hardest days. Thank you for blessing me with your trust, friendship, and excitement for this project!

INDEX

A

Aperol Spritz **330**
Apple
    Apple Cinnamon Morning Quinoa **52**
    Roasted Apple, Fennel + Yam Salad **84**
    Creamy Apple-Butternut Squash Soup **144**
    Mulligatawny Soup **160**
    Turkey-Sausage Stuffed Mushrooms **274**
    Sweet Apple + Cranberry Sauce **324**
    Creamy Apple Butternut Squash Soup **144**
    Apple Cider Vinaigrette **128**
    Apple Cider Vinaigrette, with House Mixed Greens **128**
    Apple Cranberry Sauce **324**
    Apple, Fennel + Yam Salad **84**
Almonds
    Pumpkin Chocolate Granola **50**
    Apple Cinnamon Morning Quinoa **52**
    Spiced Black Bean + Sweet Potato Salad **86**
    Romesco Sauce **304**
    Mini Coconut Almond Macaroons **356**
    Granola Bar Bites **358**
Almond Flour/Almond Meal
    Coconut Almond Crusted Chicken **182**
    Organic Greek Meatballs **192**
    Organic Turkey Meatloaf **196**
    Parmesan Crusted Chicken Fingers **212**
    Cauliflower Crust Pizza **224**
    Sarah's Best Chocolate Chip Cookies **348**
    Molten Chocolate Olive-Oil Cake **362**

Anchovy
    Green Goddess Dressing **302**
    Kale or Romaine Caesar Salad, Grilled or Classic **140**
Artichoke Hearts
    Grilled Prawn + Artichoke Salad **112**
    Healthy Spinach Artichoke Dip **276**
Arugula
    Wild Rice Salad with Grapes **104**
    Roasted Beet + Ricotta Salad **124**
Asian Chicken + Cabbage Salad **116**
Asparagus
    Pesto Chicken + Veggie Bake **186**
    Shaved Asparagus Salad **258**
Avocado
    Sarah's Everyday Green Smoothie **28**
    Peanut Butter + Date Green Smoothie **30**
    Cinnamon Green Smoothie **38**
    Photoshoot Salad **68**
    Feta + Basil Lentil Salad **70**
    Kale, Avocado + Roasted Squash Salad **72**
    Sarah's Fresh Corn Salad **100**
    Crab + Grapefruit Stuffed Avocados **102**
    Hummus Collard Wraps **106**
    Falafel Salad **114**
    The Cobb Wedge Salad **128**
    Black Bean and Spinach Enchilada Bake **198**
    Healthy Nachos **278**
    Green Goddess Dressing **302**
    Cilantro Avocado Dressing **308**
    Shredded Chicken, Avocado + Kale Quinoa Salad **134**

B

Bacon
    The Cobb Wedge Salad **128**

Banana
- Sarah's Everyday Green Smoothie 28
- Peanut Butter + Date Green Smoothie 30
- Cinnamon Green Smoothie 38
- Sarah's Basic Kale Smoothie 34
- Tropical Green Smoothie 40
- Honeydew Mint Green Smoothie 36
- Two Ingredient Pancakes 44
- Healthy Banana Bread 62
- Pistachio + Chocolate Covered Frozen Bananas 350

Baking Soda
- Flourless Carrot Cake Muffins 54
- Healthy Banana Bread 62
- Molten Chocolate Olive-Oil Cake 362

Balsamic Vinegar
- Balsamic Broiled Citrus 48
- Roasted Cherry Balsamic Chicken, Green Beans + Potatoes 202
- Easy Everyday Balsamic 296

Basil
- Zucchini + Egg McMuffins 46
- Egg, Potato + Veggie Bake 56
- Photoshoot Salad 68
- Feta + Basil Lentil Salad 70
- Kale, Avocado + Roasted Squash Salad 72
- Spinach Quinoa Bake 82
- Cold Sesame Soba Noodle Salad 88
- Cashew Pesto Kale Salad 94
- French Potato Salad 98
- Chunky Chopped Greek Salad 96
- Chopped Italian Salad 132
- Tomato Basil Soup 166
- Organic Turkey Meatloaf 196
- Quinoa Stuffed Baked Tomatoes 222
- Fried Ratatouille 228
- Shaved Asparagus Salad 258
- Green Goddess Dressing 302
- Cucumber Basil Gin + Tonics 334

Beans
- Mint + White Bean Salad 90
- Spiced Black Bean + Sweet Potato Salad 86
- Tuscan White Bean Stew 146
- Black Bean and Spinach Enchilada Bake 198
- Spiced Black Beans + Fried Plantains 220
- Healthy Baked Beans 246
- Healthy Nachos 278

Beets
- Roasted Beet + Ricotta Salad 124

Bell Pepper
- Egg, Potato + Veggie Bake 56
- Easy Roasted Vegetables 74
- Spinach Quinoa Bake 82
- Chunky Chopped Greek Salad 96
- Sarah's Fresh Corn Salad 100
- Mint + White Bean Salad 90
- Crab + Grapefruit Stuffed Avocados 102
- Hummus Collard Wraps 106
- Grilled Prawn + Artichoke Salad 112
- Poblano Quinoa Chicken Chili 148
- Coconut Corn Chowder 152
- Watermelon-Cucumber Gazpacho 156
- White Bean + Chicken Chili Verde 162
- Rustic Vegetable + Bean Chili 164
- Fajita Stir Fry 194
- Shrimp + Sausage Quinoa Paella 226
- Fried Ratatouille 228
- Fresh Spring Rolls 264
- Roasted Red Pepper Harissa Sauce 298
- Romesco Sauce 304

INDEX, CONTINUED.

Black Beans
    Spiced Black Bean + Sweet Potato Salad **86**
    Black Bean and Spinach Enchilada Bake **198**
    Spiced Black Beans + Fried Plantains **220**
    Healthy Nachos **278**
    Black Bean + Sweet Potato Salad **86**

Blueberries
    Sarah's Everyday Green Smoothie **28**

Brussel Sprouts
    Perfect Brussels Sprouts **252**

Burger
    Mini Lamb, Turkey or Beef Sliders **206**

C

Cabbage
    Asian Chicken + Cabbage Salad **116**
    Cabbage Slaw with Spicy Honey-Cilantro Dressing **138**
    Mulligatawny Soup **160**
    Classic Chicken and Vegetable Soup **170**

Caesar Salad **140**

Cake
    Molten Chocolate Olive-Oil Cake **362**

Cannellini Beans
    Mint + White Bean Salad **90**
    White Bean + Chicken Chili Verde **162**

Caprese Salad, Spanish **136**

Carrots
    Flourless Carrot Cake Muffins **54**
    Easy Roasted Vegetables **74**
    Cold Sesame Soba Noodle Salad **88**
    Asian Chicken + Cabbage Salad **116**
    Tuscan White Bean Stew **146**
    Split Pea + Carrot Soup **150**
    Hearty Lentil Stew **158**
    Rustic Vegetable + Bean Chili **164**
    Mulligatawny Soup **160**
    Classic Chicken and Vegetable Soup **170**
    Garlic-Ginger Larb Lettuce Wraps **174**
    Fresh Spring Rolls **264**

Cashew
    Cashew Pesto Kale Salad **94**
    Curry Roasted Cashews **284**

Cauliflower
    Mulligatawny Soup **160**
    Cauliflower Steaks **214**
    Cauliflower Crust Pizza **224**
    Roasted Spiced Cauliflower **254**

Cayenne Pepper
    Shredded Kale + Lentil Salad with Snap Peas and Peanut Sauce **80**

Celery
    Italian Tuna Salad **76**
    Italian-Style Egg Salad **92**
    Split Pea + Carrot Soup **150**
    Watermelon-Cucumber Gazpacho **156**
    Rustic Vegetable + Bean Chili **164**
    Classic Chicken and Vegetable Soup **170**

Cherry
    Sarah's Basic Kale Smoothie **34**
    Roasted Cherry Balsamic Chicken, Green Beans + Potatoes **202**
    Cherry Balsamic Sauce **322**

Chives
    Zucchini + Egg McMuffins **46**
    Egg, Potato + Veggie Bake **56**
    Lentil Yogurt Dip + Salad **108**
    Green Goddess Dressing **302**

Chicken
    Asian Chicken + Cabbage Salad **116**
    Mango Chicken Salad **120**

Sundried Tomato + Pulled Chicken Salad 122
Shredded Chicken, Avocado + Kale Quinoa Salad 134
Poblano Quinoa Chicken Chili 148
White Bean + Chicken Chili Verde 162
Classic Chicken and Vegetable Soup 170
Easy Shredded Chicken 234
Coconut Almond Crusted Chicken 182
Pesto Chicken + Veggie Bake 186
Organic Greek Meatballs 192
Roasted Cherry Balsamic Chicken, Green Beans + Potatoes 202
Jamaican Jerk Pineapple Chicken 208
Parmesan Crusted Chicken Fingers 212
Maple-Hot Sauce Grilled Chicken with Grilled Peaches 230

Chocolate
Sarah's Best Chocolate Chip Cookies 348
Pistachio + Chocolate Covered Frozen Bananas 350
Granola Bar Bites 358
Molten Chocolate Olive-Oil Cake 362

Chopped
Chunky Chopped Greek Salad 96

Cilantro
Spiced Black Bean + Sweet Potato Salad 86
Sarah's Fresh Corn Salad 100
Crab + Grapefruit Stuffed Avocados 102
Falafel Balls 114
Asian Chicken + Cabbage Salad 116
Cilantro Lime + Ginger Dressing 314
Cabbage Slaw with Spicy Honey-Cilantro Dressing 138
Coconut Corn Chowder 152
Grilled Flank Steak with Chimichurri Sauce + Blanched Green Beans 200
Roasted Cherry Balsamic Chicken, Green Beans + Potatoes 202
Grilled Fish with Mango Jalapeño Pineapple Salsa 232
Roasted Carrots or Parsnips with Honey, Cilantro + Lime 242
Fresh Spring Rolls 264
Healthy Nachos 278
Cilantro Avocado Dressing 308
Herbed Chimichurri 318

Cinnamon
Cinnamon Green Smoothie 38
Two Ingredient Pancakes 44
Pumpkin Chocolate Granola 50
Apple Cinnamon Morning Quinoa 52
Flourless Carrot Cake Muffins 54
Healthy Banana Bread 62
Peaches + Cream on Steel-Cut Oats or Morning Quinoa 64
Jamaican Jerk Pineapple Chicken 208
Twice-Baked Cinnamon Sweet Potatoes 260
Curry Roasted Cashews 284
Spiced Sweet Potato Chips 290
Sweet Apple + Cranberry Sauce 324
Strawberry Rhubarb Crisp 352
Granola Bar Bites 358

Coconut Flakes
Pumpkin Chocolate Granola 50
Coconut Almond Crusted Chicken 182
Curry Roasted Cashews 284
Mini Coconut Almond Macaroons 356

INDEX, CONTINUED.

Coconut Milk
- Coconut Whipped Cream 326
- Vanilla Chia Seed Pudding 58
- Peaches + Cream on Steel-Cut Oats or Morning Quinoa 64
- Shredded Kale + Lentil Salad with Snap Peas and Peanut Sauce 80
- Coconut Corn Chowder 152
- Peanut Sauce 320

Coconut Oil
- Pumpkin Chocolate Granola 50
- Apple Cinnamon Morning Quinoa 52
- Healthy Banana Bread 62
- Peaches + Cream on Steel-Cut Oats or Morning Quinoa 64
- Coconut Almond Crusted Chicken 182
- Roasted Nutmeg Delicata Squash 238
- Twice-Baked Cinnamon Sweet Potatoes 260
- Healthy Party Mix 282
- Curry Roasted Cashews 284
- Coconut Oil Popcorn 286
- Spiced Sweet Potato Chips 290
- Sarah's Best Chocolate Chip Cookies 348
- Strawberry Rhubarb Crisp 352
- Granola Bar Bites 358

Coconut Water
- Peanut Butter + Date Green Smoothie 30
- Sarah's Basic Kale Smoothie 34
- Tropical Green Smoothie 40
- Honeydew Mint Green Smoothie 36

Collard Greens
- Hummus Collard Wraps 106

Cookies
- Sarah's Best Chocolate Chip Cookies 348
- Sarah's Peanut Butter Cookies 354
- Mini Coconut Almond Macaroons 356
- Granola Bar Bites 358
- Homemade Ice Cream Cake with Cookie Crunch 360

Corn
- Coconut Corn Chowder 152
- Healthy Nachos 278

Cucumber
- Cinnamon Green Smoothie 38
- Photoshoot Salad 68
- Italian Tuna Salad 76
- Cold Sesame Soba Noodle Salad 88
- Chunky Chopped Greek Salad 96
- Mint + White Bean Salad 90
- Crab + Grapefruit Stuffed Avocados 102
- Hummus Collard Wraps 106
- Grilled Prawn + Artichoke Salad 112
- Falafel Salad 114
- The Cobb Wedge Salad 128
- Mediterranean Spinach Salad 130
- Watermelon-Cucumber Gazpacho 156
- Fresh Spring Rolls 264
- Cucumber Hummus Boats 270
- Cucumber Yogurt Dressing 300
- Cucumber Basil Gin + Tonics 334

Chai
- Chai-Infused Whiskey 344

Chia Seeds
- Sarah's Basic Kale Smoothie 34
- Pumpkin Chocolate Granola 50
- Apple Cinnamon Morning Quinoa 52
- Flourless Carrot Cake Muffins 54
- Vanilla Chia Seed Pudding 58
- Healthy Banana Bread 62
- Falafel Balls 114
- Organic Turkey Meatloaf 196
- Sarah's Best Chocolate Chip Cookies 348
- Sarah's Peanut Butter Cookies 354

Chickpeas
- Photoshoot Salad 68
- Falafel Balls 114

Chili
- Poblano Quinoa Chicken Chili **148**

Chili Powder
- Spinach Quinoa Bake **82**
- Mulligatawny Soup **160**
- Shrimp + Sausage Quinoa Paella **226**

Chimmichurri
- Grilled Flank Steak with Chimichurri Sauce + Blanched Green Beans **200**
- Herbed Chimichurri **318**

Cranberry
- Sweet Apple + Cranberry Sauce **324**

Cobb Wedge Salad **128**

Cocoa Powder
- Pumpkin Chocolate Granola **50**

Corn
- Sarah's Fresh Corn Salad **100**
- Black Bean and Spinach Enchilada Bake **198**
- Coconut Oil Popcorn **286**

Corn Tortillas
- Black Bean and Spinach Enchilada Bake **198**
- Healthy Nachos **278**

Cucumber
- Cinnamon Green Smoothie **38**
- Photoshoot Salad **68**
- Italian Tuna Salad **76**
- Cold Sesame Soba Noodle Salad **88**
- Chunky Chopped Greek Salad **96**
- Mint + White Bean Salad **90**
- Crab + Grapefruit Stuffed Avocados **102**
- Hummus Collard Wraps **106**
- Grilled Prawn + Artichoke Salad **112**
- Falafel Salad **114**
- The Cobb Wedge Salad **128**
- Mediterranean Spinach Salad **130**
- Watermelon-Cucumber Gazpacho **156**
- Fresh Spring Rolls **264**
- Cucumber Hummus Boats **270**
- Cucumber Yogurt Dressing **300**
- Cucumber Basil Gin + Tonics **334**

Cumin
- Flourless Carrot Cake Muffins **54**
- Spiced Black Bean + Sweet Potato Salad **86**
- Sarah's Fresh Corn Salad **100**
- Fajita Stir Fry **194**
- Jamaican Jerk Pineapple Chicken **208**
- Spiced Black Beans + Fried Plantains **220**
- Spiced Sweet Potato Chips **290**
- Roasted Red Pepper Harissa Sauce **298**

Curry
- Mulligatawny Soup **160**
- Butternut Squash, Salmon + Vegetable Curry **180**
- Curry-Spiced Sweet Potato Fries **250**
- Curry Roasted Cashews **284**

D

Dates
- Peanut Butter + Date Green Smoothie **30**
- Moroccan Lamb or Veggie Stew **168**
- Roasted Spiced Cauliflower **254**
- Sweet Apple + Cranberry Sauce **324**

Dijon Mustard
- Kale, Avocado + Roasted Squash Salad **72**
- Italian Tuna Salad **76**
- Italian-Style Egg Salad **92**
- Mustard Roasted Fish + Fennel **188**
- Organic Greek Meatballs **192**

INDEX, CONTINUED.

Dijon Mustard (continued)
    Organic Turkey Meatloaf **196**
    Healthy Baked Beans **246**

Dill
    French Potato Salad **98**
    Chunky Chopped Greek Salad **96**
    Split Pea + Carrot Soup **150**
    Organic Greek Meatballs **192**
    Cucumber Yogurt Dressing **300**

E

Eggs
    Two Ingredient Pancakes **44**
    Zucchini + Egg McMuffins **46**
    Egg, Potato + Veggie Bake **56**
    Healthy Banana Bread **62**
    Spinach Quinoa Bake **82**
    Italian-Style Egg Salad **92**
    The Cobb Wedge Salad **128**
    Organic Greek Meatballs **192**
    Organic Turkey Meatloaf **196**
    Pizza Quinoa Bites **210**
    Cauliflower Crust Pizza **224**
    Sarah's Peanut Butter Cookies **354**
    Mini Coconut Almond Macaroons **356**
    Molten Chocolate Olive-Oil Cake **362**

Egg Salad **92**

Eggplant
    Eggplant Bolognese Lasagna **178**
    Fried Ratatouille **228**

Enchiladas
    Black Bean and Spinach Enchilada Bake **198**

F

Fajitas
    Fajita Stir Fry **194**

Falafel
    Falafel Salad **114**

Fennel
    Roasted Apple, Fennel + Yam Salad **84**
    Falafel Salad **114**
    Mustard Roasted Fish + Fennel **188**

Feta + Basil Lentil Salad **70**

Feta Cheese
    Feta + Basil Lentil Salad **70**
    Kale, Avocado + Roasted Squash Salad **72**
    Wild Rice Salad with Grapes **104**
    Falafel Salad **114**
    Sundried Tomato + Pulled Chicken Salad **122**
    Spiced Black Beans + Fried Plantains **220**
    Healthy Nachos **278**

Fish
    Mustard Roasted Fish + Fennel **188**
    Fajita Stir Fry **194**
    Molasses Ginger Salmon **204**
    Grilled Fish with Spring Pea + Mint Puree **216**
    Grilled Fish with Mango Jalapeño Pineapple Salsa **232**

Flour, gluten free
    Healthy Banana Bread **62**

French Potato Salad **98**

Frozen Bananas
    Pistachio + Chocolate Covered Frozen Bananas **350**

Fruit Crisp
    Strawberry Rhubarb Crisp **352**

G

Garam Masala
    Flourless Carrot Cake Muffins **54**

Garbanzo Beans
    Photoshoot Salad **68**
    Falafel Balls **114**
    Chopped Italian Salad **132**
    Mediterranean Spinach Salad **130**
    Moroccan Lamb or Veggie Stew **168**

Garlic
    Egg, Potato + Veggie Bake 56
    Easy Roasted Vegetables 74
    Spinach Quinoa Bake 82
    Falafel Balls 114
    Kale or Romaine Caesar Salad, Grilled or Classic 140
    Tomato Basil Soup 166
    Moroccan Lamb or Veggie Stew 168
    Garlic-Ginger Larb Lettuce Wraps 174
    Organic Turkey Meatloaf 196
    Grilled Flank Steak with Chimichurri Sauce + Blanched Green Beans 200
    Roasted Cherry Balsamic Chicken, Green Beans + Potatoes 202
    Quinoa Stuffed Baked Tomatoes 222
    Shrimp + Sausage Quinoa Paella 226
    Fried Ratatouille 228
    Olive Oil Mashed Potatoes with Garlic + Herbs 240
    Roasted Spiced Cauliflower 254
    Healthy Baked Beans 246
    Roasted Potato Bites with Chive-Parsley Tapenade 272
    Roasted Red Pepper Harissa Sauce 298
    Herbed Chimichurri 318
    Romesco Sauce 304

Gin
    Cucumber Basil Gin + Tonics 334
    Sage Gin Fizz 336

Ginger
    Cilantro Lime + Ginger Dressing 314
    Moroccan Lamb or Veggie Stew 168
    Mulligatawny Soup 160
    Garlic-Ginger Larb Lettuce Wraps 174
    Butternut Squash, Salmon + Vegetable Curry 180
    Molasses Ginger Salmon 204

Goat Cheese
    Zucchini + Egg McMuffins 46
    Mango Chicken Salad 120
    Sundried Tomato + Pulled Chicken Salad 122
    Black Bean and Spinach Enchilada Bake 198
    Turkey-Sausage Stuffed Mushrooms 274

Grains
    Wild Rice Salad with Grapes 104

Grapefruit
    Balsamic Broiled Citrus 48
    Crab + Grapefruit Stuffed Avocados 102
    Fresh Grapefruit Greyhound 342

Grapes
    Wild Rice Salad with Grapes 104

Green Beans
    Pesto Chicken + Veggie Bake 186
    Grilled Flank Steak with Chimichurri Sauce + Blanched Green Beans 200
    Roasted Cherry Balsamic Chicken, Green Beans + Potatoes 202

Green Goddess Dressing 302

Green Onion
    Cold Sesame Soba Noodle Salad 88
    Lentil Yogurt Dip + Salad 108
    Grilled Prawn + Artichoke Salad 112

Greyhound
    Fresh Grapefruit Greyhound 342

INDEX, CONTINUED.

H

Honey
    Balsamic Broiled Citrus **48**
    Toasted Mochi with Peanut Butter + Honey **60**
    Peaches + Cream on Steel-Cut Oats or Morning Quinoa **64**

    Shredded Kale + Lentil Salad with Snap Peas and Peanut Sauce **80**
    Cilantro Lime + Ginger Dressing **314**
    Honey Cilantro Dressing, Spicy **138**
    Roasted Carrots or Parsnips with Honey, Cilantro + Lime **242**
    Honey Mustard Poppy Seed Dressing **310**
    Peanut Sauce **320**
    Sarah's Peanut Butter Cookies **354**
    Mini Coconut Almond Macaroons **356**
    Honey Cilantro Dressing, Spicy **138**

Hummus
    Hummus Collard Wraps **106**
    Cucumber Hummus Boats **270**

I

Ice Cream
    Homemade Ice Cream Cake with Cookie Crunch **360**

Italian Seasoning
    Spinach Quinoa Bake **82**
    Sundried Tomato + Pulled Chicken Salad **122**

J

Jalepeño
    Grilled Fish with Mango Jalapeño Pineapple Salsa **232**
    Healthy Nachos **278**
    Roasted Red Pepper Harissa Sauce **298**
    Cilantro Avocado Dressing **308**

Jerk Chicken
    Jamaican Jerk Pineapple Chicken **208**

K

Kale
    Cinnamon Green Smoothie **38**
    Sarah's Basic Kale Smoothie **34**
    Tropical Green Smoothie **40**
    Egg, Potato + Veggie Bake **56**
    Kale, Avocado + Roasted Squash Salad **72**
    Shredded Kale + Lentil Salad with Snap Peas and Peanut Sauce **80**
    Spinach Quinoa Bake **82**
    Cashew Pesto Kale Salad **94**
    Shredded Chicken, Avocado + Kale Quinoa Salad **134**
    Kale or Romaine Caesar Salad, Grilled or Classic **140**

Kale, Avocado + Roasted Squash Salad **72**
Kale + Lentil Salad with Snap Peas and Peanut Sauce **320**

L

Lamb
    Moroccan Lamb or Veggie Stew **168**
    Mini Lamb, Turkey or Beef Sliders **206**

Lasagna
    Eggplant Bolognese Lasagna **178**

Lemon
    Flourless Carrot Cake Muffins **54**
    Photoshoot Salad **68**
    Cashew Pesto Kale Salad **94**
    Chunky Chopped Greek Salad **96**
    Mint + White Bean Salad **90**
    Hummus Collard Wraps **106**

Grilled Prawn + Artichoke Salad 112
Roasted Beet + Ricotta Salad 124
Kale or Romaine Caesar Salad, Grilled or Classic 140
Shaved Asparagus Salad 258

Mediterranean Lemon Tahini Dressing 316

Lentils
Feta + Basil Lentil Salad 70
Shredded Kale + Lentil Salad with Snap Peas and Peanut Sauce 80
Lentil Yogurt Dip + Salad 108
Hearty Lentil Stew 158

Lime
Spiced Black Bean + Sweet Potato Salad 86
Cold Sesame Soba Noodle Salad 88
Sarah's Fresh Corn Salad 100
Crab + Grapefruit Stuffed Avocados 102
Cilantro Lime + Ginger Dressing 314
Watermelon-Cucumber Gazpacho 156
Spiced Black Beans + Fried Plantains 220
Roasted Carrots or Parsnips with Honey, Cilantro + Lime 242
Cilantro Avocado Dressing 308
Sarah's Classic Healthy Margarita 338

M

Macaroon
Mini Coconut Almond Macaroons 356

Mango
Sarah's Basic Kale Smoothie 34
Tropical Green Smoothie 40
Mango Chicken Salad 120
Grilled Fish with Mango Jalapeño Pineapple Salsa 232

Maple Syrup
Pumpkin Chocolate Granola 50
Vanilla Chia Seed Pudding 58
Toasted Mochi with Peanut Butter + Honey 60
Healthy Banana Bread 62
Peaches + Cream on Steel-Cut Oats or Morning Quinoa 64
Kale, Avocado + Roasted Squash Salad 72
Roasted Cherry Balsamic Chicken, Green Beans + Potatoes 202
Maple-Hot Sauce Grilled Chicken with Grilled Peaches 230
Healthy Baked Beans 246
Sarah's Peanut Butter Cookies 354

Margarita
Sarah's Classic Healthy Margarita 338

Mashed Potatoes
Olive Oil Mashed Potatoes with Garlic + Herbs 240

Meatloaf
Organic Turkey Meatloaf 196

Melon
Honeydew Mint Green Smoothie 36

Milk
Peaches + Cream on Steel-Cut Oats or Morning Quinoa 64

Mint
Honeydew Mint Green Smoothie 36
Mint + White Bean Salad 90
Watermelon-Cucumber Gazpacho 156
Grilled Fish with Spring Pea + Mint Puree 216
Shaved Asparagus Salad 258
Fresh Spring Rolls 264
Cucumber Yogurt Dressing 300

INDEX, CONTINUED.

Mixed Greens
    Falafel Salad **114**
    Mixed Greens with Apple Cider Vinaigrette **126**
Mochi
    Toasted Mochi with Peanut Butter + Honey **60**
Molasses
    Molasses Ginger Salmon **204**
    Healthy Baked Beans **246**
Mozzarella
    Spanish Caprese Salad **136**
    Eggplant Bolognese Lasagna **178**
    Pesto Chicken + Veggie Bake **186**
    Pizza Quinoa Bites **210**
Mushroom
    Egg, Potato + Veggie Bake **56**
    Hearty Lentil Stew **158**
    Shrimp + Sausage Quinoa Paella **226**

N

Nachos
    Healthy Nachos **278**
No Bake Cookies
    Granola Bar Bites **358**
Nutritional Yeast
    Cashew Pesto Kale Salad **94**

O

Oats, Steel Cut
    Peaches + Cream on Steel-Cut Oats or Morning Quinoa **64**
    Strawberry Rhubarb Crisp **352**
Olives
    Chunky Chopped Greek Salad **96**
    Spanish Caprese Salad **136**
    Moroccan Lamb or Veggie Stew **168**
Onion
    Zucchini + Egg McMuffins **46**
    Egg, Potato + Veggie Bake **56**
    Spinach Quinoa Bake **82**
    Roasted Apple, Fennel + Yam Salad **84**
    Chunky Chopped Greek Salad **96**
    Crab + Grapefruit Stuffed Avocados **102**
    Falafel Balls **114**
    Poblano Quinoa Chicken Chili **148**
    Watermelon-Cucumber Gazpacho **156**
    Tomato Basil Soup **166**
    Moroccan Lamb or Veggie Stew **168**
    Rustic Vegetable + Bean Chili **164**
    Fajita Stir Fry **194**
    Organic Turkey Meatloaf **196**
    Mini Lamb, Turkey or Beef Sliders **206**
    Healthy Baked Beans **246**
Orange
    Spiced Black Bean + Sweet Potato Salad **86**
Oregano
    Chunky Chopped Greek Salad **96**

P

Paella
    Shrimp + Sausage Quinoa Paella **226**
Pancakes
    Two Ingredient Pancakes **44**
Parmesan Cheese
    Photoshoot Salad **68**
    Pesto Chicken + Veggie Bake **186**
    Pizza Quinoa Bites **210**
    Parmesan Crusted Chicken Fingers **212**
    Grilled Fish with Spring Pea + Mint Puree **216**
    Cauliflower Crust Pizza **224**
    Spinach, Pea + Parmesan Bowls **256**

Parmesan Crisps with Roasted Tomatoes **268**
Turkey-Sausage Stuffed Mushrooms **274**
Healthy Spinach Artichoke Dip **276**

Parsley
Egg, Potato + Veggie Bake **56**
Spiced Black Bean + Sweet Potato Salad **86**
French Potato Salad **98**
Grilled Prawn + Artichoke Salad **112**
Falafel Balls **114**
Classic Chicken and Vegetable Soup **170**
Mini Lamb, Turkey or Beef Sliders **206**
Olive Oil Mashed Potatoes with Garlic + Herbs **240**
Shaved Asparagus Salad **258**
Roasted Potato Bites with Chive-Parsley Tapenade **272**
Herbed Chimichurri **318**

Parsnips
Roasted Carrots or Parsnips with Honey, Cilantro + Lime **242**

Pasta
Zucchini Pasta Noodles **184**
Baked Spaghetti Squash **190**

Peach
Peaches + Cream on Steel-Cut Oats or Morning Quinoa **64**
Maple-Hot Sauce Grilled Chicken with Grilled Peaches **230**

Peanuts
Asian Chicken + Cabbage Salad **116**
Healthy Party Mix **282**
Peanut Sauce **320**

Peanut Butter/Almond Butter
Peanut Butter + Date Green Smoothie **30**
Toasted Mochi with Peanut Butter + Honey **60**
Shredded Kale + Lentil Salad with Snap Peas and Peanut Sauce **80**
Sarah's Peanut Butter Cookies **354**
Granola Bar Bites **358**

Peas
Split Pea + Carrot Soup **150**
Butternut Squash, Salmon + Vegetable Curry **180**
Grilled Fish with Spring Pea + Mint Puree **216**
Shrimp + Sausage Quinoa Paella **226**
Spinach, Pea + Parmesan Bowls **256**

Pesto
Pesto Chicken + Veggie Bake **186**
Pesto Kale Salad **94**

Photoshoot Salad **68**

Pickles
Italian-Style Egg Salad **92**

Pineapple
Tropical Green Smoothie **40**
Jamaican Jerk Pineapple Chicken **208**
Grilled Fish with Mango Jalapeño Pineapple Salsa **232**

Pistachios
Mango Chicken Salad **120**
Pistachio + Chocolate Covered Frozen Bananas **350**

Pizza
Pizza Quinoa Bites **210**
Cauliflower Crust Pizza **224**

Plantains
Spiced Black Beans + Fried Plantains **220**

Popcorn
Coconut Oil Popcorn **286**

Poppy Seed
Honey Mustard Poppy Seed Dressing **310**

Potatoes
Egg, Potato + Veggie Bake **56**
French Potato Salad **98**
Tuscan White Bean Stew **146**

INDEX, CONTINUED.

Potatoes (continued)
    Rustic Vegetable + Bean Chili **164**
    Olive Oil Mashed Potatoes with Garlic + Herbs **240**
    Smashed Potatoes **248**
    Roasted Potato Bites with Chive-Parsley Tapenade **272**

Prosecco
    Aperol Spritz **330**
    Prosecco + St. Germaine with Strawberries **332**

Pumpkin Seeds
    Pumpkin Chocolate Granola **50**

Q

Quinoa
    Apple Cinnamon Morning Quinoa **52**
    Peaches + Cream on Steel-Cut Oats or Morning Quinoa **64**
    Spinach Quinoa Bake **82**
    Shredded Chicken, Avocado + Kale Quinoa Salad **134**
    Poblano Quinoa Chicken Chili **148**
    Pizza Quinoa Bites **210**
    Quinoa Stuffed Baked Tomatoes **222**
    Shrimp + Sausage Quinoa Paella **226**
    Spinach, Pea + Parmesan Bowls **256**

R

Radish
    Cold Sesame Soba Noodle Salad **88**
    Healthy Nachos **278**

Raisins
    Apple Cinnamon Morning Quinoa **52**

Rhubarb
    Strawberry Rhubarb Crisp **352**

Rice
    Wild Rice Salad with Grapes **104**

Rice Cereal
    Healthy Party Mix **282**

Rice Paper
    Fresh Spring Rolls **264**

Rice Wine Vinegar
    Cold Sesame Soba Noodle Salad **88**

Ricotta Cheese
    Egg, Potato + Veggie Bake **56**
    Roasted Beet + Ricotta Salad **124**

Roasted
    Roasted Vegetables **242, 254**
    Roasted Beet + Ricotta Salad **124**

Romaine Lettuce
    Peanut Butter + Date Green Smoothie **30**
    Honeydew Mint Green Smoothie **36**
    Hummus Collard Wraps **106**
    Falafel Salad **114**
    Mango Chicken Salad **120**
    Chopped Italian Salad **132**

S

Salad
    Photoshoot Salad **68**
    Feta + Basil Lentil Salad **70**
    Kale, Avocado + Roasted Squash Salad **72**
    Easy Roasted Vegetables **74**
    Italian Tuna Salad **76**
    Sesame Snap Peas **78**
    Shredded Kale + Lentil Salad with Snap Peas and Peanut Sauce **80**
    Spinach Quinoa Bake **82**
    Roasted Apple, Fennel + Yam Salad **84**
    Spiced Black Bean + Sweet Potato Salad **86**
    Cold Sesame Soba Noodle Salad **88**
    Italian-Style Egg Salad **92**

Salad (continued)
- Cashew Pesto Kale Salad **94**
- Chunky Chopped Greek Salad **96**
- Sarah's Fresh Corn Salad **100**
- Grilled Prawn + Artichoke Salad **112**
- Falafel Salad **114**
- Asian Chicken + Cabbage Salad **116**
- Mango Chicken Salad **120**
- House Mixed Greens with Apple Cider Vinaigrette **126**
- The Cobb Wedge Salad **128**
- Kale or Romaine Caesar Salad, Grilled or Classic **140**
- Spanish Caprese Salad **136**
- Mediterranean Spinach Salad **130**

Salmon
- Butternut Squash, Salmon + Vegetable Curry **180**
- Molasses Ginger Salmon **204**

Seafood
- Crab + Grapefruit Stuffed Avocados **102**
- Grilled Prawn + Artichoke Salad **112**
- Molasses Ginger Salmon **204**
- Shrimp + Sausage Quinoa Paella **226**

Sesame Oil, toasted
- Sesame Snap Peas **78**
- Cold Sesame Soba Noodle Salad **88**
- Cilantro Lime + Ginger Dressing **314**
- Molasses Ginger Salmon **204**
- Healthy Party Mix **282**

Sesame Seeds
- Cold Sesame Soba Noodle Salad **88**
- Asian Chicken + Cabbage Salad **116**

Shredded Kale + Lentil Salad with Snap Peas and Peanut Sauce **80**

Shrimp
- Shrimp + Sausage Quinoa Paella **226**

Simple Syrup
- Homemade Healthy Simple Syrup **337**

Snap Peas
- Sesame Snap Peas **78**

Spinach
- Sarah's Everyday Green Smoothie **28**
- Peanut Butter + Date Green Smoothie **30**
- Cinnamon Green Smoothie **38**
- Spinach Quinoa Bake **82**
- Mediterranean Spinach Salad **130**
- Black Bean and Spinach Enchilada Bake **198**
- Quinoa Stuffed Baked Tomatoes **222**
- Spinach, Pea + Parmesan Bowls **256**
- Healthy Spinach Artichoke Dip **276**

Spinach Artichoke Dip **276**
Spinach Salad, Mediterranean **130**
Spinach Quinoa Bake **82**

Squash
- Kale, Avocado + Roasted Squash Salad **72**
- Easy Roasted Vegetables **74**
- Roasted Apple, Fennel + Yam Salad **84**
- Creamy Apple Butternut Squash Soup **144**
- Butternut Squash, Salmon + Vegetable Curry **180**
- Baked Spaghetti Squash **190**
- Fried Ratatouille **228**
- Roasted Nutmeg Delicata Squash **238**

St Germaine
- Prosecco + St. Germaine with Strawberries **332**

INDEX, CONTINUED.

Steak
- Grilled Flank Steak with Chimichurri Sauce + Blanched Green Beans **200**
- Cauliflower Steaks **214**

Strawberry
- Strawberry Rhubarb Crisp **352**

Stuffed Mushrooms
- Turkey-Sausage Stuffed Mushrooms **274**

Sundried Tomato
- Sundried Tomato + Pulled Chicken Salad **122**

Sundried Tomato + Pulled Chicken Salad **122**

Sunflower Seeds
- Healthy Party Mix **282**

Sugar
- Flourless Carrot Cake Muffins **54**
- Healthy Banana Bread **62**

Sweet Potato
- Roasted Apple, Fennel + Yam Salad **84**
- Spiced Black Bean + Sweet Potato Salad **86**

Sweet Potato (continued)
- Moroccan Lamb or Veggie Stew **168**
- Curry-Spiced Sweet Potato Fries **250**
- Twice-Baked Cinnamon Sweet Potatoes **260**
- Spiced Sweet Potato Chips **290**

T

Tahini
- Mediterranean Lemon Tahini Dressing **316**

Tamari Sauce
- Shredded Kale + Lentil Salad with Snap Peas and Peanut Sauce **80**
- Asian Chicken + Cabbage Salad **116**
- Cilantro Lime + Ginger Dressing **314**
- Peanut Sauce **320**

Tequila
- Sarah's Classic Healthy Margarita **338**

Tomatoes, baby/grape/cherry
- Photoshoot Salad **68**
- Feta + Basil Lentil Salad **70**
- Italian Tuna Salad **76**
- Spinach Quinoa Bake **82**
- Grilled Prawn + Artichoke Salad **112**
- Falafel Salad **114**
- The Cobb Wedge Salad **128**
- Spanish Caprese Salad **136**
- Mediterranean Spinach Salad **130**
- Moroccan Lamb or Veggie Stew **168**
- Rustic Vegetable + Bean Chili **164**
- Eggplant Bolognese Lasagna **178**
- Mini Lamb, Turkey or Beef Sliders **206**
- Quinoa Stuffed Baked Tomatoes **222**
- Shrimp + Sausage Quinoa Paella **226**
- Fried Ratatouille **228**
- Parmesan Crisps with Roasted Tomatoes **268**
- Cucumber Hummus Boats **270**
- Roasted Red Pepper Harissa Sauce **298**

Tuna
- Italian Tuna Salad **76**

Turkey, ground
- Garlic-Ginger Larb Lettuce Wraps **174**
- Eggplant Bolognese Lasagna **178**
- Organic Greek Meatballs **192**
- Organic Turkey Meatloaf **196**
- Mini Lamb, Turkey or Beef Sliders **206**

Turkey, ground (continued)
- Quinoa Stuffed Baked Tomatoes **222**
- Turkey-Sausage Stuffed Mushrooms **274**

Tzaziki Sauce
- Cucumber Yogurt Dressing **300**

Y

Yams
- Roasted Apple, Fennel + Yam Salad **84**
- Spiced Black Bean + Sweet Potato Salad **86**
- Curry-Spiced Sweet Potato Fries **250**
- Twice-Baked Cinnamon Sweet Potatoes **260**
- Spiced Sweet Potato Chips **290**

Yogurt, whole milk
- Spinach Quinoa Bake **82**
- Lentil Yogurt Dip + Salad **108**
- Cilantro Lime + Ginger Dressing **314**
- Cabbage Slaw with Spicy Honey-Cilantro Dressing **138**
- Healthy Spinach Artichoke Dip **276**
- Cucumber Yogurt Dressing **300**

W

Watermelon
- Watermelon-Cucumber Gazpacho **156**

Walnuts
- Flourless Carrot Cake Muffins **54**
- Healthy Banana Bread **62**
- Wild Rice Salad with Grapes **104**

Wedge Salad **128**

Whiskey
- Chai-Infused Whiskey **344**

White Beans
- Mint + White Bean Salad **90**
- White Bean + Chicken Chili Verde **162**
- Rustic Vegetable + Bean Chili **164**
- Healthy Baked Beans **246**

Wild Rice
- Wild Rice Salad with Grapes **104**
- Quinoa Stuffed Baked Tomatoes **222**
- Shrimp + Sausage Quinoa Paella **226**

V

Vanilla
- Coconut Whipped Cream **326**
- Pumpkin Chocolate Granola **50**
- Flourless Carrot Cake Muffins **54**
- Vanilla Chia Seed Pudding **58**
- Healthy Banana Bread **62**
- Sarah's Best Chocolate Chip Cookies **348**

Vodka
- Fresh Grapefruit Greyhound **342**

Z

Zucchini
- Zucchini + Egg McMuffins **46**
- Easy Roasted Vegetables **74**
- Poblano Quinoa Chicken Chili **148**
- Zucchini Pasta Noodles **184**
- Fried Ratatouille **228**